Early Regard for *Sleep, Pray, Heal*

Donna Fado Ivery's book is a beautiful story rising out of a beautiful life. I read it with joy.

—John Shelby Spong,
>Bishop Emeritus of the Episcopal Diocese of Newark
>Author of 30 books, with over a million sold

A "must read" for anyone experiencing chronic pain. This masterpiece is a poignant, deeply personal guidebook for clergy and care-givers who are in ministry with people on the journey of disability. It is a treasure-trove of inspiration, good advice, and it is a refreshing testimony to the power of God, who brings light and life to the depths of human suffering.

—Peggy A. Johnson,
>Bishop of the Philadelphia Area of The United Methodist Church and Former Pastor of Christ UMC of the Deaf in Baltimore, Maryland

Sleep, Pray, Heal is a remarkable chronicle of a journey bordered by deep and relentless pain, and yet buoyed by the constant presence of the Spirit. Each page, each poem, each painting is a prayer – often rising from loss and anguish – but never apart from a profound trust embracing the searching love of God. I was moved and challenged.

—Gordon Light,
>Retired bishop, Anglican Church of Canada

A great gift to all who have experienced pain—and who hasn't? The author's memoir is vivid and her grasp of spiritual sources shines light through the darkness. Her creative use of art in the quest for healing is unique and impressive.

    —J. Philip Wogaman,
        Former Pastor of President Clinton and Former
        Dean of Wesley Seminary, Washington D.C.

Exquisite! Donna Fado Ivery describes her journey with unrelenting pain, and shares hard and hopeful truths about living with that pain and traveling with the Spirit. She offers the great gift of herself and her spiritual journey, evoking quiet tears and big smiles in this reader. The artistry of the book and the author will speak powerfully to readers living with chronic pain in themselves and others. The book reveals the power of seeking life, crying out to God, and trusting the Spirit, while recognizing and celebrating the small and mighty blessings along the way. It is a very human and spiritual gift—a treasure.

    —Mary Elizabeth Moore,
        Dean and Professor
        Boston University School of Theology

I found *Sleep, Pray, Heal* to be a profound dispatch from the spiritual frontier. Donna has written an account of spiritual depths that is deeply moving and instructive for us all. I do not know when I have encountered personal experience so faithfully and winningly interpreted through biblical and theological reflection and artistic expression.

—**Neal F. Fisher,**
President Emeritus, Garrett-Evangelical
Theological Seminary in Evanston, Illinois

It has been a privilege to have been a clergy colleague of the Rev. Donna Fado Ivery for more than twenty years now and to have watched her live her faith through her long journey of dealing with her brain injury and chronic pain toward healing. *Sleep, Pray, Heal* is a beautifully and powerfully written book, where the Rev. Fado Ivery unfolds for us her theological thinking on so many issues of life, including sexism, racism, interracial marriage, suffering and pain, and faith in God. Each story is touching and speaks to the heart and mind. What a model of doing theology autobiographically this book is! What a gift she has given us!

—**Kah-Jin Jeffrey Kuan,**
President and Professor of Hebrew Bible
Claremont School of Theology

Life, accident, pain, and dependence on prescription medication could happen to anyone. That's why this story of overcoming years of pain and medication is a must read! Reverend Donna Fado Ivery's words in *Sleep, Pray, Heal: A Path to Wholeness and Well-Being* led me to see how easy it could be for one person to slip into the statistics of our nation's opioid crisis.

I will definitely make an order for my Sunday School class.

You will be inspired by her true and beautiful story of triumph and unconditional love as she made her way out of the pit and was healed, and you will want to share her story.

—Lynette Renee Grandison, M.D.
Stanislaus Medical Society President 2018–2019

Donna Fado Ivery's book, *Sleep, Pray, Heal: A Path to Wholeness and Well-Being* is a modern sermon on faith— a beautifully articulated, joy-based sermon, full of ups and downs—imbued with an uplifting sense of the miraculous.

—Linda Watanabe McFerrin,
Author of *Namako, The Hand of Buddha*,
and *Navigating the Divide*

Donna Fado Ivery has a storyteller's gift, and a profound story to tell: a fateful accident that changes everything, a spouse's love that endures all things, two children to live and to fight for, a faith that buoys her, courage that equips for the long journey to recovery, paints and canvas that grant new depth to her voice, the Holy Spirit who works through the brushes. A book to be read, savored and shared. This will serve as an important resource for church groups and other communities who support survivors of trauma.

> **—Shelly Matthews,**
> Professor of New Testament,
> Brite Divinity School

In Sleep, Pray, Heal, Donna Fado Ivery manages to give a bizarre accident universal meaning, telling an unfathomable story in a way that invites readers to understand our own lives, our own sufferings, through new eyes. She confronts her searing pain proactively, by insisting on truth, invoking—even demanding—the tangible presence of the Holy Spirit, and engaging the dynamic outlet of art for expression. This is a practical guide, an inspirational journal, and a fascinating story to be read more than once, for inspiration, challenge, direction and peace.

> **—Susan Hunn,**
> United Methodist Lay Person and Nonprofit
> Administrator

Sleep, Pray, Heal: A Path to Wholeness and Well-Being is one of the most compelling books I have read in a long time. I was equally moved by her paintings which occupy this book, as I was by her eloquent writing. I kept it by my bed, where I read it before sleeping and picked it up first thing in the morning because I couldn't bear to go stretches without reading it. What happened to Donna Fado Ivery could have happened to anyone. But not just anybody could have written *Sleep, Pray, Heal: A Path the Wholeness and Well-Being*. I cannot recommend it highly enough. I learned so much reading it. It grabbed my heart and never let go.

> **—Catherine DeMonte,**
> Psychotherapist and Author of *Beep! Beep! Get Out of My Way!: Seven Tools for Living Your Unstoppable Life*

Every three years I fall in love with a book. *Sleep, Pray, Heal* is my three-year book.

> **—Carol Krane,**
> Lifelong Learner

This book is for you and those who care about you: if you have suffered a life-changing brain injury and are trying to heal; if you suffer from chronic pain that has diminished your functioning and joy, if you are feeling alone in your suffering and lack a positive vision for your future; if you are feeling spiritually bereft and disconnected from God and are struggling to reconnect for the first time.

When life-changing injuries and chronic pain occur, everyone in the patient's orbit is affected. There can be confusion about how to help, about why the person isn't getting better, or why the person seems pretty good one day and a mess the next. As a person struggles, their vision of their future can become clouded and confused. As for many in Rev. Fado Ivery's situation, healing is a journey that teaches and demands patience. When a person's life is turned upside down, the resulting existential crisis may exceed what humans can do. There are times in my work when prayer and spiritual guidance are crucial to a patient's healing.

I strongly encourage professionals in healing fields, pastors, and leaders of healing ministries to use and share *Sleep, Pray, Heal* with those who are seeking wholeness and well-being for themselves and those who are striving to help them.

> **—Dr. Jen Tellier,**
> Neuropsychologist
> Alameda, California

Author's Note

The paintings in *Sleep, Pray, Heal: A Path to Wholeness and Well-Being* are an important part of my story. The colors of each painting express nuance, vibrancy, and feeling. Because color would double the cost of the print book, *Sleep, Pray, Heal* is printed in black and white. While the eBook has color images, eBooks are not configured in a way that translate images effectively. I also want to make the images available to audiobook listeners.

Without color, the images sing like a solo instead of a full chorus. I hope that you will visit my website and download the pdf of *Sleep, Pray, Heal Color Images*. These can easily be printed on any home printer and tucked in the book.

Donna Fado Ivery

www. DonnaFadoIvery.com

A Path to Wholeness and Well-Being

Sleep
Pray
Heal

DONNA FADO IVERY

ADVENTURES IN HEALING

Adventures In Healing Sacramento
www.AdventuresInHealing.com

The author of this book does not dispense medical advice or prescribe the use of any technique, either directly or indirectly, as a form of treatment for physical, emotional, or medical problems, without the advice of a physician. The intent of this author is only to offer information of a general nature to help you in your quest for emotional and spiritual well-being. In the event you use any of the information in this book for yourself, which is your constitutional right, the author and the publisher assume no responsibility for your actions.

ISBN 978-1-7336399-5-8

Scripture quotations are within Gratis Use copyright guidelines.

Editor: Linda Watanabe McFerrin
Cover art: Donna Fado Ivery

First printing 2019

Publisher's Cataloging-in-Publication Data

Names: Ivery, Donna Fado, author.
Title: Sleep , pray , heal : a path to wholeness and well-being / Donna Fado Ivery.
Description: Sacramento, CA: Adventures in Healing, 2019.
Identifiers: LCCN 2019905888 | ISBN 978-1-7336399-5-8
Subjects: LCSH Ivery, Donna Fado. | Brain damage--Patients--Rehabilitation--Biography. | Brain damage--Patients--Biography. | Chronic pain--Patients--United States--Biography. | Methodist Church--Clergy--Biography. | Disabilities--Religious aspects--Christianity. | Prayer. | Spiritual healing. | Brain damage--Alternative treatment. | Art therapy. | BISAC BIOGRAPHY & AUTOBIOGRAPHY / Personal Memoirs | RELIGION / Christian Living / Inspirational | HEALTH & FITNESS / Healing | BODY, MIND & SPIRIT / Healing / Prayer & Spiritual
Classification: LCC RC387.5 .I84 2019 | DDC 617.4/8104430092--dc23

For Hubert, Aisha, Imani, Don and Jean,
and the Spirit who uplifts, sustains and restores.

Contents

PART I: BREAKING OPEN

1: Fallen..2

2: Shadows of Saint Francis...............................6

3: Angels Watching Over Me.............................28

4: A Love Story - Boston, Massachusetts............ 35

5: Desert Dwelling...65

PART II: PAINTING PRAYERS

6: Too Deep for Words....................................82

7: Uncovering...89

8: Healing Headache..95

9: Beautiful Mess 102

10: Rocking Lost.. 115

11: Possibly Never...139

12: Coloring Family..148

13: Hopes Dashed... 156

14: Broken Yet Whole.................................... 171

15: Formed by Tears......................................189

16: Barely There..197

17: Dormant..205

PART III: CREATING ANEW

18: Watershed..212

19: Dancing with Pain....................................227

20: The Storm of a Lawsuit.............................246

21: Pruning 268

22: Finding Balance...................................... 282

23: Morning Star Rising.................................292

24: Circle Dance... 310

Epilogue.. 321

Acknowledgments..322

Author's Invitation and Website.....................325

References & Permissions..............................326

Scripture Translations..................................334

Scripture Index..335

PART I: BREAKING OPEN

O sabbath rest of Galilee!
O calm of hills above,
where Jesus knelt to share with thee
the silence of eternity interpreted by love.
Drop thy still dews of quietness till all our striving cease;
take from our souls the strain and stress,
and let our ordered lives confess the beauty of thy peace.

> *John Greenleaf Whittier, 1872*
> *Dear Lord and Father of Mankind*
> *From his poem, "The Brewing of Soma"*

1: FALLEN

January 26, 1994

"WOULD IT BE POSSIBLE FOR US to have a table with a view?"
I ask. My husband Hubert, in-laws Leroy and Eula, and
daughters—four-year old Aisha and nine-month old Imani—
are together on vacation and we are primed and ready to
celebrate with a fancy meal. Twenty-two miles long and
twelve miles wide, Lake Tahoe's azure waters are really
something to behold.

"Sure," the hostess answers as she picks up a stack of
leather-bound menus and leads us through a maze of aisles.

As I walk through the restaurant, I see that my question
is moot. The lakeside exterior wall is glass. Interior frameless
glass partitions, one after the other, create a seemingly seamless
long glass wall that affords lakeside views at each table, as
well as acoustic division. Two rows of dark wood and burnt
orange leather booths transect the long room and create
aisles. The foot of each glass partition is set into wood molding
on the back of each booth, the tops mounted to the ceiling.
Smaller tables that seat parties of four and two are sprinkled
throughout. The design of the restaurant relays an ambience
of woodsy elegance. *So fancy!*

1: Fallen

"You guys should sit where you can see the view." I offer the view seating to Eula and Leroy as I slide into the booth with my back facing the lake and scoot over next to the high chair on my right. Hubert is putting Imani in the high chair. Eula, Leroy, and Aisha are about to sit down. An earsplitting bellow stops them.

The falling plate glass roars like rumbling thunder. The very air protests with a siren maelstrom. The first strike of lightning hits its target, the base of my skull.

"BOOM."

My head is forced forward. Instantaneously I brace it by holding onto my face as if I'm sobbing into my hands, covering my eyes and cheeks with my open palms. The glass partition hits the table top in front of me and rebounds.

"WAM."

Its second lightning strike hits the left side of my head, just above my ear, and then slams onto the table in front of me. Amber glasses of ice water shatter, spewing jagged shards, cracked ice, and pools of water.

As if a bomb has completed its mission, the uproar stops. The over two-hundred-pound glass partition, five feet high by eight feet wide, and one-half inch thick, has separated from its ceiling moorings, fallen, and hit me twice on the head.

Silence.

Within the quiet beneath, at the very base of who I am,

my soul-self spontaneously cries out. *Jesus, save me!*

In the ensuing hush I hear my own screams, an encore to the wailing protests of the air surrounding me.

Earthquake, I instantly construe, and believe the building has come down around us.

My gush of screams transmutes into words. "Where's the baby?! Where's the baby?! My baby!" Imani should be in the high chair just to my right. *Don't pass out. You can't pass out*, I tell myself. I should be able to reach her, but I can't move. I am pinned down, smashed down, by the glass wall.

Hubert's voice comes to me, like a life preserver tossed toward a drowning woman. "Donna! Donna! Everyone's okay."

Tumbling out like a raft careening down the rapids, I scream, "Get it off me! Get it off me!"

Hubert's booming voice calls out, "Somebody help me get this off her!"

I have never heard him yell so loudly. Weird that he needs help. He is so strong.

One time at church, three men together carried a heavy pottery statue downstairs to a lower-level multipurpose room. Not having seen their struggle, Hubert merely lifted the same statue above his head and carried it back up the same stairs.

The smashing pressure lifts, but I don't dare move. My

1: Fallen

closed fists dig into the hollow just below my cheekbones, hitchhiker thumbs support my chin, my elbows a kickstand on the table top to stabilize my head and neck. If my neck is broken, I could be paralyzed.

Don't move. Don't move.

"Somebody call an ambulance!" Hubert yells out in an alarming voice, and then sits down next to me. Under the table, I feel his hand on my knee, tethering my trembling to his solid presence.

Fear fills me. I know I've been severely injured. What about my family? I want to survive.

2: SHADOWS OF SAINT FRANCIS

January 13, 1994 (two weeks before)

THE OAK EXECUTIVE DESK IS LARGER than any I have ever worked behind. Grasping the arms of the desk chair, I push myself up to almost standing and reach to the opposite side of the desk for a stack of books. It's quite a stretch. The roomy senior pastor's office of the Madera United Methodist Church is ideal for small group meetings. It is professionally appointed with two walls of built-in bookcases, a blue upholstered swivel rocker, accent chairs, end table, lamp, clean beige carpet and matching draperies. None of the furnishings are new, but they are all in good shape. The woods throughout match and are finished beautifully. I imagine that someone in the church was a carpenter and donated his time. Everything is clean and polished, because there is a custodian on staff who comes in to dust and vacuum, a first for me.

At first glance, most any resident of this traditional San Joaquin Valley of California town will think me an odd fit for my job: age thirty-two, five-foot nine, with brown hair cut just below the ear and fair skin usually pink from the sun, I'm not the traditional pastor. The biggest reach, though, is that I am a woman. This is compounded by yet another:

I am married to the associate pastor who happens to be a towering six-foot-seven African American man. It used to be a reach for me to kiss Hubert, too, but now I'm used to it. Only six months ago at this church the senior pastor fit the traditional mold: a respected older white male whose lovely wife worked primarily with youth and children as Christian Education Director. Then we were hired and sent: first woman minister, first interracially married pastor, first African American associate pastor, first gender reversal of senior and associate pastoral roles. So many firsts are a reach and require transition time for everyone involved: for the community, for my family, and, of course, for me. I feel responsible, and more than a little worried. Down the hall, the personnel committee is meeting to evaluate the work of both pastors and whether to request that we remain come July 1st, when pretty much all clergy move in the United Methodist system. Hubert and I, each in our respective offices, await their decision. *Perhaps having me and Hubert as pastors has been too far of a reach for them. That would certainly be understandable. There are so many adjustments that they need to make.*

Hubert and I have been here only six months, barely enough time to settle in. Each January, United Methodist Churches and clergy submit their pastoral requests to the presiding bishop, and what the bishop says goes for the annual "appointment," or where each clergy person will serve/work beginning July 1st. Clergy can refuse a church, and churches can refuse a pastor, but that's frowned upon, and would greatly influence future appointments. As an elder, something like having tenure, I am guaranteed a full time pastoral position somewhere in Northern California or Nevada, the geographical area of my presiding bishop. Madera United Methodist Church (UMC), was my bishop's choice, and I think it was a good one.

An ache of apprehension builds in me. *What is taking them so long?* I expected them to be done with their assessment and decision well over an hour ago. With the unexpected length of their meeting, I prepare myself for the worst, an official vote that can be translated as, "We don't want you." I envision the falling domino chain of negative consequences, the downward spiral of professional mobility, setback of salary, loss of home, upset of our daughters—three-year-old Aisha and newborn Imani—slowdown of Hubert's Ph.D. program, and the work of needing to move again. But with all that, the part that hurts the most is, "We don't want you."

The Christian ministry is not just a job, it's deeply, intimately woven within who I am. I am fortunate to have been raised within a loving family. My dad was a United Methodist pastor and my mom a singer/actress/musician turned supportive minister's wife and homemaker. Religion gave me the language and ritual to nurture and understand the spiritual in me.

My parents tell me that one of the earliest displays of

my personality was as a one-year-old riding a plastic horse on four wheels. To this day I remember my favorite toy clearly, hollowed plastic in pastel yellow, blue, and white, with curly hair, big black eyes, dowel handles, and sculpted saddle. The first time they put me on it, I immediately took off—fast—with glee. I rode on the front porch, a cement slab without railings, about twelve-by-six feet, with a sheer eighteen-inch drop-off to the grass below. *I'd take it right to the edge and not fall off*, tilting and turning with wheels that don't turn, the noisier, the faster, the better.

How did I *learn* to race my plastic horse? *I didn't.* Nobody taught me. I was too young to have learned how to ride at breakneck speed by figuring it out and practicing. My intuition came *before* my learning or experiencing.

In his classic work, *Critique of Pure Reason (1781)*, the great philosopher Immanuel Kant unpacked the problems inherent in rationalism versus empiricism, or in other words, the volleying argument, "I think because I feel," and "I feel because I think," popular in the Age of Enlightenment. Kant proposed a deeper knowing *a priori*, (that comes before), a faculty of consciousness that is transcendental and intuitive. He regarded faith and soul as essential. At the seat of it all is a divine reality.

Which comes first, the chicken or the egg? My answer is God, *a priori*. The first two verses of the Holy Bible recount the order:

In the beginning God created
the heavens and the earth.
And the earth was waste and void;
and darkness was upon the face of the deep
and the Spirit of God moved
upon the face of the waters.

Genesis1:1-2 (ASV)

In the beginning, God. Then, God's Spirit moved upon the inky abyss, the formless void, the deep waters, the black hole, and created the heavens and the earth. The Spirit, moving, is the most powerful element on earth and in heaven.

A priori from experience or reason, the movement of the Spirit is a sacred, creative gust of God's breathing that connects us to the innermost seed of who we are, to our very soul-selves. The magnetic pull of the Spirit is like a concerto's deep bass notes that ground the higher notes into the fullness of exquisite harmony. The transcendent, divine spark of the Spirit draws us into alignment with who we are born to be. *My life purpose is not to see what will move me, but for the Spirit of God to move in me.*

The most memorable moments of my life are when I fall into who God designed me to be, and am carried by the movement of the Spirit. It's as if the earth moves, intuition takes over, and I'm forever imprinted by the experience.

Junior High School was a lesson in humiliation for me. As I walked down the main corridor where swarms of students rushed to their next class, some of the boys routinely announced my presence by barking.

As much as school deflated me, church youth group buoyed me. Through Bible study, laughter, games, retreats, and service projects, we learned to be Christian among our peers in a supportive social environment. Living in Fresno, only an hour from Yosemite, taking a five-day High Sierra backpacking trip with the youth group was the highlight of each summer.

When I was in ninth grade and backpacking with the youth group, I hiked by myself up, up, and further up a steep rocky trail. High above the timberline, I sat down on the mountainside and looked out upon the vast wonder of creation. *Breathtaking.* I remember the variegated carpet of trees below, vista of rolling mountain ranges, stretch of sky and clouds beyond measure, and warmth of smooth granite beneath my palms. So very high up where trees cannot grow, rocks bake without shade. I prayed and relaxed and only then noticed inches from my hand a flower growing in the smallest amount of soil in the crevice of the granite. I was amazed that a flower could bloom where nothing else can grow. I was literally *awestruck.* The Spirit of the Living God spoke to me through that flower on the mountain. *The life of Jesus is like this, blooming in whatever rock hard circumstance. You will do the same.*

This was an *a priori* moment, when God breaks through and reveals who we really are. I dove into the life altering current, no holds barred, and let the Spirit carry me.

The Spirit is carrying me now. Nine months ago a beautiful baby girl, Imani, was added to our family of Aisha, age three, Hubert, and me. Only two weeks after having the baby we received a surprise phone call that the bishop would like us to move to Madera and begin our new positions in less than three months. Hubert would leave his job as chaplain at the Fred Finch Youth Center, a United Methodist residential treatment facility in Oakland. He would take new jobs as both the part-time solo pastor of the St. Mark's United Methodist Church, a small Black Church in Fresno, and part-time associate pastor at the Madera United Methodist Church. I would leave my job as solo pastor at the Wesley United Methodist Church in Hayward to be senior pastor at the Madera United Methodist Church. At three weeks post birth, we interviewed for the positions and then rushed to find a mortgage broker and buy our first home. We sold our Chevy Impala used for in-town trips of less than three miles and bought a car good for distance driving. It's not so much that it was a *good* car, the used Eagle was the only car we could quickly find that fit both Hubert's tall frame and our growing family. Our old gas-guzzler would probably not have made the three-hour drive from Hayward to Madera.

So, only two work weeks after returning from my six-week maternity leave, I said goodbye to my beloved church family where I had pastored for the last five years. We moved from a smaller church in a larger town to a larger church in a smaller town. We moved from the liberal metropolitan San Francisco Bay Area to a pretty much homogeneous traditional rural community. We moved from culturally diverse Hayward, where English is a second language in public schools in which many of the students speak almost a hundred different languages and dialects at home, to Madera where public schools offer Spanish-English bilingual tracks. In Madera there is a cultural and racial divide, with Latinos living on one side of the freeway, and white folk, our home and church on the other side, with a sprinkling of diversity throughout. Madera is the county seat, and large enough to have a new Walmart. For the first time Hubert and I would work together on the same staff, which means we will need to develop a whole new game plan to preserve home space as separate from work space within our relationship. All of these changes comprised a list of lifetime event stressors that happened in the course of three months.

Of course, the move is also a blessing. I thoroughly enjoy working at the Madera United Methodist Church and with its members: hungry in faith, extraordinary in kindness, strong in community, exceptional in volunteering. What more could a pastor desire? *Not much at all.* I enjoy having a role like the CEO of a company, the half-million-dollar budget and staff, the family-oriented fulcrum of Madera. Kids are welcome everywhere. There are so many young families at this church, not just because this church is larger than our last, but because in this town, families *do church*. I've been able to add working out at the athletic club to my regular routine because they provide free childcare. Taking step aerobics class three times a week and playing racquetball with other young moms is a blast, and the girls love playing in the provided nursery. I've been able to lose the baby weight. We have a healthy, balanced lifestyle here.

And, the church has been nothing but flexible and supportive to our family's needs. In Hayward, the tiny pastor's office had two doors, one to the secretary's office and the other to a large nursery. For part of my office hours, Aisha napped and played in a glorious playroom. We were able to manage our work hours in such a way that Aisha was in infant childcare or preschool three days per week, the weekends with Daddy, one weekday off with Mommy, and one weekday at work with Mommy. Because Madera is so family-oriented, even with Hubert now working weekends, we have been able to keep Aisha on a three-day-per week preschool schedule, plus keep the baby breastfeeding and out of childcare altogether.

In Madera, the church office is a bustling place. Because Hubert's and my offices are a mere four feet away from one another's, and only two miles from home, we've been able to stagger our work hours. I usually nurse the baby at home and arrive to the church at 7:00 AM so that I have a few quiet work hours alone before the office opens. Hubert brings the baby to me at the office for her midmorning feeding and nap, and then I take her home at lunchtime so that Hubert has his turn, sans kids at the office. It's been no problem having a baby crawling around the floor during staff meetings. The pastoral offices open onto the main office and reception area, and the carpet is kept clean by the church custodian. There is usually a volunteer receptionist who loves to have a baby on her lap for twenty minutes or so. We are able to work from both home and church. Because Hubert and I share equally in child raising and homemaking, and the church is amazingly flexible, we are able to manage a baby swap lifestyle rather seamlessly. It's never okay to bring along a child when visiting the hospital or providing pastoral care to someone in crisis, but it's great to bring along a young one when making pastoral calls to nursing homes and the homebound, and I love to do worship planning with a baby on my lap. Imani coos, blows spit bubbles, and is rapt during what she perceives is story time for her alone. She has an affinity for traditional church music. When I was pregnant and leading worship, Imani danced in utero whenever the organ resounded. Lately her favorite game is to crawl as fast as she can between our offices, strike a pose with an adorable smile, get me or Hubert to smile, and then race back to the other parent.

Another blessing of our move is that our salaries increased. For the most part, churches do not raise their pastors' pay or even give a cost-of-living increase, and the way to increase income in a ministerial career is to move. We bought plane tickets for Hubert's parents, who live in Florida, to visit. They arrive this Saturday and will spend two weeks of vacation with us. We were able to buy a sofa bed for them to sleep on, the first purchase of new furniture in our marriage. At the New Years Day sale, I also bought a four-poster pine bed with dressers and nightstands, and then with the "cash award," bought a living room chaise and bedding. Zero percent interest, to be paid off in a year. I had phoned Hubert to see if he wanted to come to the store and check it out, and he said whatever I pick out is fine. *Cool. He is so easy going.* We had been using the nightstands and dressers from the children's French Provincial canopy bedroom set I shared with my sister in the second grade.

The Madera United Methodist Church has the biggest sanctuary in town, and preaching to a crowd is *exhilarating.* It's what I do best. Even amidst the strong positives in our move to Madera, however, we had concerns at once. The hardest struggles to deal with are those that I experience like a punch to the gut and keep me up at night.

Moving into our older ranch-style house in Madera, a neighbor greeted us, saying, "It's a good thing the neighbors sharing your back fence moved away last year. He was the

2: Shadows of Saint Francis

Grand Dragon of the KKK." Returning her smile, nodding my head in agreement, I successfully covered up the lead cannonball dating back to the Civil War that had just landed on me.

Parking the car to pick up Aisha from preschool, I watched her sad and alone on the play yard. She was dragging a rock in the dirt, trying to look occupied while the other children laughed and played together. Aisha has always, quite naturally, played well with other children. The ferocious Mama Bear in me reared to protect her cub, but I talked myself down. *She just needs more time to make new friends.* But when my just-turned-four-year-old daughter talked about niggers at the kitchen table, I high-tailed it to the preschool to discuss the problem with the director. She informed me that Aisha had learned the word from somewhere else, that their preschool is Christian and teaches about God's love through Bible stories. Although I was seated, the Mama Bear in me stood tall for a fight. I tried to speak gently and firmly, but the shake and volume of my voice, the steely glare of my eyes, and grinding grip of my jaw betrayed my cover. "Shame on you!" I blurted. And then with only a smidgen of control I said, "If you can't see a problem, you can't fix it. I am withdrawing her immediately." Hurriedly I stood and exited the director's office. I didn't shake her hand. I didn't say goodbye. Making a beeline to the classroom, I plastered on a fake smile and spoke to Aisha as if we were talking about

17

Santa Claus. "Get your things, Aisha, you get to come to work with Mommy today."

Once Aisha was safely strapped into her child seat, I closed the car door, leaned back against it, and took a moment to regroup. Tilting my face to the sun, I breathed deeply to steady my rage. I felt ashamed that I had given naysayers about women in ministry something more to talk about. And talk they do.

In Hayward I was just one of the crowd, not so in Madera. When I go to the grocery store with my milk-chocolate-skinned girls, I stand out. Some people give me glares of racial indignation. Some whisper with curiosity and others with disdain. "She must be that new Methodist pastor." Others make a point to tell me how beautiful my daughters are, or how pleased they are that I'm a preacher and have moved to town. A few people have told me how nice it is that I have adopted children. I'm living in a fishbowl, never knowing when someone will walk by to take a look, to stare, to check me out.

I'm also in a profession where I'm on display. For many in the congregation who were open to "trying out" a woman minister, in the pulpit is where I prove that I can be, and become "pastor." For the visitors who "just came by to hear a female preach," I feel a need to prove that women can and will do it well.

Women needing to prove themselves is nothing new in

Christianity. Some of the most coveted treasures of the church are steeped in appalling sexism. The Bible is chock-full of wonderful words of life as well as archaic cultural contexts in scripture verses that include polygamy, slavery, and women as unclean, chattel, weak, immoral, and subordinate to men. Christians have finally reached the era that we are of one mind that slavery is not the will of God, even though the scriptures can be interpreted as the opposite:

> *Slaves, obey your earthly masters*
> *with fear and trembling,*
> *in singleness of heart,*
> *as you obey Christ.*
>
> *Ephesians 6:5 (NRSV)*

We have not yet reached consensus on the appalling texts regarding women.

I have hope in the church because the Spirit of God continues to move, to melt hearts, to create anew, to break the chains of bondage. *I will never give up on the Spirit.* I haven't given up on the church, a body and language of the body of Christ, a channel of the grace and love of God. Church tradition is full of treasures, like Saint Augustine (354-430) who wrote a shockingly transparent biography of his life and revealed how the Spirit led him on a journey— emotional, physical, spiritual, theological, and intellectual— to discover:

My heart is restless until it finds its rest in thee.
> *The Confessions of Saint Augustine,*
> *Book 1, Paragraph 1*

He also revealed his ongoing, deep-seated problems with women in his life, and how conquering sexuality and women was the way to spiritual purification.

> *The woman together with her husband is the image of God, so that that whole substance is one image. But when she is assigned as a helpmate, a function that pertains to her alone, then she is not the image of God; but as far as the man is concerned he is by himself alone the image of God, just as fully and completely as when he and the woman are joined together into one*
>
> > *Saint Augustine (354–430)*
> > *On the Trinity, Book 12, Chapter 7*

The Bible also contradicts Saint Augustine:

> *So God created humankind in his image,*
> *in the image of God he created them;*
> *male and female he created them.*
>
> > *Genesis 1:27 (NRSV)*

Women in ministry continually need to prove themselves. An old-wise-woman saying, "Don't throw out the baby with the bathwater," applies to the church's misogynist tradition that threatens to obscure the life within. There's a treasure—a baby—in the smelly bathwater of the church. I will never let go of the precious Living Lord, Jesus. *Yes, Lord, my heart is restless until it finds its rest in thee.*

My encounter with the preschool director placed me on high alert. We moved Aisha to a non-religious preschool and she did well there. I decided I needed a therapist, but didn't want someone projecting the traditional roles of pastor and mother onto me. I didn't want to see a therapist in town where people would talk when I came out of her office. I wanted someone with the fewest assumptions possible who could help me unpack *stuff*. I found the right one in nearby Fresno: a womanist, Jewish counselor with a strong academic background. She was able to call me on my tendency to approach difficult situations with my mind first, and then let the heart catch up. She encouraged me to create a home that is an oasis for my family.

An intellectual approach has always come easily to me. The drawback of my mind-first approach is that I'm not very vulnerable. Answering God's call for me to enter the ministry was to choose a life where I would grow the most, in a vocation that focuses on the matters of the heart and faith, which are always deeper and broader than knowledge.

Now faith is confidence in what we hope for and assurance about what we do not see.

Hebrews 11:1 (NIV)

I need all of that faith now.

We've been waiting for a long time, *too long.* The heaviness of my lactating breasts alerts me that it is past time to nurse Imani and get her to bed. She and Aisha are in the nursery on the far side of the church grounds. Aisha, forever the helpful big sister, is able to translate Imani's baby babble, distract her with play, and soothe away her tears. The babysitter, provided by the church anytime there are night meetings, is great, too. Right now I'm probably the only one uncomfortable.

I dislike being evaluated. The committee could share with accolades a dozen things I do well, and what will stick with me is the one "growing edge." *Admit it, deep down you are a perfectionist.* Someway, somehow, I move through this life as if its foundation is a simple equation of logic: to work harder plus find a way to do better equals everything will work out. The inverse is assumed to be true: to work less plus not do better equals everything will fall apart. *That's a recipe for an overachiever.* The Protestant Work Ethic is a recipe for an overachiever as well. If I am evaluated as not doing my best, at the most deeply-seated part of me, I feel as though my world will fall apart, that my discipleship has slacked. At my very base, I have a fear of failure.

2: Shadows of Saint Francis

My knee-jerk reaction to the surfacing emotion of fear is to get to work. This Sunday I will preach the biography of Saint Francis of Assisi. I was raised with the role model of one of the best preachers I've ever heard, my dad. Delivered in first person with feeling and without notes, the Reverend Don Fado's biographical sermons connect to real life and this is how I like to preach as well. Very little invigorates me more than preaching strong in the Spirit.

Standing up halfway, I reach far across to the corner of the massive desk for a stack of books on Saint Francis of Assisi. Although I've already memorized my manuscript and devoured these books on his life, I thumb through them again. Opening myself to the witness of Saint Francis, I allow some of his experiences to drift down through the surface of my consciousness to the deeper, feeling spaces within me. Born in 1181 in Italy, Francis was a wealthy, popular, and rambunctious young man destined to live a carefree life. He fought as a soldier, was taken prisoner for a year, and then after returning to a life of ease in Assisi, was taken ill for a year. During his imprisonment and illness he was sorely tested. I can imagine bored Francis noticing the movement of the shadows across his room and then looking forward to their dependable, timely greeting. I can imagine depressed Francis establishing a relationship with the shadows and beginning to call the sun his brother and the moon his sister. I can imagine lonely Francis enjoying his talks with the little bird who visited him each day. His time of testing was a time of conversion to follow Jesus in peace and service, to live in harmony with nature and animals, and to rely completely upon the blessings of God for sustenance. The Prayer of Saint Francis is a song of his heart.

> *Lord, make me an instrument of your peace.*
> *Where there is hatred, let me sow love,*
> *Where there is injury, pardon*
> *Where there is doubt, faith*
> *Where there is despair, hope,*
> *Where there is darkness, light,*
> *Where there is sadness, joy.*
> *O Divine Master, grant that we may not so much*
> *Seek to be consoled as to console*
> *To be understood as to understand*
> *To be loved as to love*
> *For it is in giving that we receive*
> *It is in pardoning that we are pardoned*
> *And it is in dying that we are born to eternal life.*
>
> *The Prayer of Saint Francis*
> *Attributed to Saint Francis of Assisi*

The *Prayer of Saint Francis* helps me to approach center, where the weight of the world is held in balance. For me, prayer doesn't wipe the slate clean or remove offending weights. Prayer operates more like an old fashioned weighing scale, where a beam rests on a central fulcrum and makes a way to discover true balance of mass and force and whatever's real. Now centered, the echo of imagining, "We don't want you," drifts through me, unearthing feelings of shame and failure.

I prop my elbows on the desk, my temples in my fists, and pray. *Lead me, Lord. You never said that following you would be easy. No matter what happens, I know that your love will sustain me.*

Prayer stills and quiets me.

Like a bundle dropped by a stork from on high, words are delivered to my mind and heart. Jesus preached that we are not to worry. God watches over, clothes, and feeds the birds of the air and flowers in the field, and God provides for us, too. The lyrics and tune of the gospel hymn, "His Eye Is on the Sparrow," strum through me, and I hum along.

Why should I feel discouraged,
  why should the shadows come,
Why should my heart be lonely,
  and long for heaven and home,
When Jesus is my portion,
  my constant friend is He:
His eye is on the sparrow,

and I know He watches me;
His eye is on the sparrow,
and I know He watches me.
I sing because I'm happy,
I sing because I'm free.
His eye is on the sparrow,
and I know He watches me.

Words by Civilla D. Martin, 1905
Music by Charles H. Gabriel, 1905

I open my new *The Message Bible*, within easy reach on my desk, to revisit the classic, "Do not worry" teachings of Jesus, and see how Eugene Peterson has translated the original Greek into modern day language. The last verse of the passage is like an ibuprofen to a sprained ankle, cough syrup to a hacking fit, comfort to my anxiety.

Give your entire attention to what God is doing right now, and don't get worked up about what may or may not happen tomorrow. God will help you deal with whatever hard things come up when the time comes.

Matthew 6:34 (MSG)

As soon as I'm at peace with whatever will be, the knock comes at the door. I grab my sweater and put it on over my dress, more a layer of protection than to keep me warm, and then open the door. The chairman of the personnel committee says, "We're ready for you."

Hubert comes out of his office and we walk together down the long hallway. Late at night the corridor is empty and the click of my heels echoes and sounds ominous. The chairman escorts us to the meeting room where eight committee members, both men and women, sit around a conference table. We take our seats at the table.

The chairman says, "Donna and Hubert, we have taken the time to fully discuss our decision, and we are happy to say that the vote is unanimous. We want you to continue as our pastors."

My whole body relaxes, my breast milk lets down, drips through my bra and onto my dress.

Little did I know that the shadows of Saint Francis would soon surround me.

3: Angels Watching Over Me

January 26, 1994 (the day of injury)

THE SOUNDS OF THE SLOT MACHINES announce our entry to the casino in Stateline, Nevada. The clink-clink-clink of coins dropping into metal trays, the ding-ding-ding of winning bells, and a periodic yell of excitement overshadow the silence of mesmerized adults gathered to play.

Stunned by the chaos of new sounds and lights, nine-month-old Imani snuggles into the crook of her daddy's neck. Aisha is interested in this new environment. She stares at it all as she walks a little more closely than usual by my side, her security cemented by holding onto my hand.

"Lordy, daughter, this is something!" Leroy says to me, shaking his head back and forth.

Eula has a sparkle in her eye. She is enjoying the new sights and sounds.

Neither of them have been in a casino before. Identifying the array of fruit trees lining the California freeway, tasting the sweet harvest purchased in the fruit stands, tending the fire to heat their Miami bones, and of course, being with their eldest son, Hubert, daughter-in-law, and granddaughters are their delight.

3: Angels Watching Over Me

We have been staying in a nearby mountain cabin for the last three days. With dark wood siding and forest green trim, the 1940s rustic mountain cabin in the Lake Tahoe community of Meyers, Nevada, *should* be great. Owned by a church member, the picturesque cabin was loaned to us for our three weeknight stay in Lake Tahoe. With a bedroom downstairs for my in-laws and space for Hubert, me, and our daughters upstairs, yellowed knotty-pine paneling, wood burning stove to heat the living room, and small kitchen, the quaint cabin *should be perfect* for our vacation. Grandpa Leroy has gladly taken on the chore of tending the fire and guarding the hot metal from little children. The cabin is a place of constant baby patrol, with Mama-always-on-watch tension. Upon our arrival to the cabin, we discovered that water in the pipes had frozen and one needed to be replaced. After driving to the hardware store for a replacement pipe and cleaning the mice droppings out from under the sink, Hubert laid on the floor to fix it.

During Imani's nap time this morning, Eula and Leroy babysat while Hubert and I took Aisha out to play in the snow. We drove around the forested neighborhood to look for a small hill to try out our plastic saucer. We couldn't seem to find a hill to glide down, which is like saying you can't find a straw of hay in a haystack. Our tires spun on an icy steep street, and we gathered branches to get traction. In a labyrinth of winding streets, we looked for a sign, any sign to help us get our bearings. The street sign said, "Lost Lane." We were lost on Lost Lane.

We were still basking in relief from the church asking us to remain as pastors. We are basking in the joy of having family here. Today my parents drove their motorhome up the mountain to meet us for lunch at a popular snow sledding site. As Aisha and I sailed down the hill in plastic saucers and played in the snow, the rest of my family watched and visited with coffee, leftovers, sandwiches, and cocoa in the warmth of the RV. *Such a wonderful time.*

I enjoy being with Hubert's parents. Their depth of calm and relaxed loving presence is obvious. I suspect that there are not many Black folk who would accept with open arms a White daughter-in-law. Hubert's love is broad like a mountain meadow. His parents, Eula and Leroy, love in a similar way.

Eula, a loving mother of eight children, a nurse's assistant, is a woman with a warm and open heart, an ever-ready twinkle in her eye, and a mischievous sense of humor. She loves to care for her gaggle of grandchildren, loves to keep up with her soaps and phone buddies, and play the numbers. Leroy, known as Pop Ivery to the Miami, Dade County neighborhood, is the fatherly figure upon whom the community relies. Pop Ivery is the guy who makes sandwiches for any passerby in need, tends his magnificent garden, and shares a listening ear and sage advice. Enjoying the Miami warm breeze, Leroy would relax in the front yard with an empty seat ready for folks to drop by to talk or eat, and the seat is rarely empty. Pop Ivery didn't have time for church with his many jobs to provide for his family and took the Lord's day to rest, and he needed to keep an eye on his house because, Lord knows, a house routinely empty on Sundays is a magnet for folks up to no good. At heart, Leroy was a preacher. *God, I give you thanks for my family. Bless them. Keep them safe. In Jesus' name, I pray.*

Tonight is the one meal we will eat out this week as part of our strategy to clean the kitchen. Today we eat leftovers to empty the refrigerator. Tomorrow morning we will thoroughly clean the rustic place just before we leave. Because of the weather report my parents chose not to stay to have dinner with us. They drove the two hours down the mountain to Sacramento before the storm hit. As soon as we get in the car and start our drive to the casino for dinner out, the storm begins. The drive is harrowing with snowfall and limited visibility. Everything seems to be going wrong. I focus on the positive to deflect the negative. It's just too special to have family gathered around.

A dozen people are ahead of us to meet the hostess at the entrance to the casino restaurant. Strategically placed slot machines invite playing as we wait in line. Advertisements for $5.99 prime rib lure tourists into the casino.

"Eula, I brought a roll of quarters. Wanna play?"

"Um hmm. Thought you'd never ask!" she replies with

a twinkle in her eye.

We are entertained by the gambling console and one another, hooting, giggling and cutting-up like teenage girls over a game in the video arcade.

"Mommy, can I play?" Aisha asks, now holding onto Grandaddy Leroy's hand.

"No, honey. Only adults can touch these machines, because it's gambling."

The last quarter deposited and lost in the coin slot coincides with our reaching the hostess perched behind a polished wood podium that could be a pulpit with a shiny brass light.

"How many in your party?" she asks, in a courteous, but perfunctory way.

"Five and a high chair," Hubert answers.

That is when my world caves in.

Hubert's voice has returned to his quiet, lapping stream tone. "Stay still, Donna. The ambulance is coming." But its slightly higher pitch betrays his panic.

Two ambulance EMTs help me to move from sitting to lying on the gurney. They strap me to the backboard and immobilize my head and neck with padding blocks and more straps. Standing far enough away so as not to interfere, my family watches. Aisha, weeping quietly, is held in her Grandaddy's arms. I want to console her with words of assurance that everything will be alright, but I can't because I could be lying, and that would be worse for her than tears. Grandma Eula holds Imani who sucks on her fist as if it were a pacifier.

On a gurney, rolling through the casino, I am captivated by the ceiling lights. There are so many of them creating a fake atmosphere wherein day is indistinguishable from night. I share a similar disjointed reality, a bizarre sense of shock. Reality seems to have rolled out of reach.

When we reach the ambulance, Hubert bends over, looks me in the eye, and speaks to me loudly, slowly, clearly, "Donna, I'm going to drive the car, and follow the ambulance to the hospital. We will all be there with you."

"Yes," I whisper.

One EMT drives and the other sits in the back of the ambulance with me.

"Donna, my name is Mike. We're going to get you to the hospital so that you can be checked out, okay?"

In a rattly voice I answer, "Okay,"

"I'm going to ask you a few questions."

I blink the affirmative.

"Can you tell me your name?"

"Donna Fado Ivery."

"Do you know what year it is?"

"1994."

"Do you know who the president is?"

"Clinton."

The radio, the siren, the flashing red lights, and my new best friend, Mike, all seem to skirt the surface of my reality. I'm in limbo, propelled like a hovercraft skating above choppy waters.

Mike chats with the other EMT. "Did you see how heavy that thing was?"

"That glass was so thick, no wonder it didn't break."

"I can't believe she's conscious."

"She must have some angels watching over her."

4: A Love Story
Boston, Massachusetts 1984-93

SHEETS OF RAIN ANGLED by the afternoon wind pelted the old sidewalks and Victorian brick townhouses along Bay State Road, a block from the Charles River in Boston. The picturesque dorms of Boston University line the street, usually accentuated by students, but not today. People had sought refuge from the storm that hailed like cats and dogs scampering and fighting.

Plumping my two bed pillows to cover the wooden arms of the love seat, I lay down across it to get comfortable to watch TV. Three housemates sat properly in matching chairs, designed for institutional wear, not comfort. Ten residents from the US and one from Africa live together in the Theology House. It's a running joke that they can tell I'm from California because I do such things as say hello to strangers on the street, and sprawl out and get comfortable in the community living room.

A knock at the front door called me to leave my nest, and answering the door, I was met by an extremely tall man with ebony skin who was sopping wet. Wearing a newsboy style hat and navy blue trench coat, his umbrella was wrong-side out, and water dripped off of his eyelashes, high cheekbones, and chin. A prospective student, he was sent by recruitment to stay in the one empty bed in the Theology House. I took his coat and hat, hung them to dry, and fixed him a cup of tea.

While he warmed up and dried off, we all visited and learned he was a Baptist minister from Houston, Texas. He had driven up—Yikes, what a long drive—to look at the Psychology and Ethics doctoral program. Hubert Ivery courteously answered our barrage of questions: He is six foot seven. He received his Masters of Divinity degree at the Interdenominational Theological Center (ITC), the Graduate School of Religion of Morehouse University in Atlanta. Yes, he played basketball in college. Yes, he is asked that question frequently. Yes, the ring he wears is a championship ring; he played in college, Texas Southern University, and they won the NAIA National Championship. My first impression of Hubert Ivery was that he is a Southern gentleman, soft spoken, very tall, and super skinny.

I had no idea that I had just met my soulmate.

Over summer break the Theology House moved to a taller and three times wider building a few blocks down Bay State Road, within earshot of Fenway Park. The Victorian brownstone had been perpetually deemed an "Animal House." Boston University had recently designated it for graduate theology students as a strategy to eliminate property damage and drug abuse This past summer the house was completely renovated with a new large kitchen for our cooperative cooking meal plan.

Lugging my heavy suitcase, before the invention of wheels on suitcases, from the airport, to the "T"—Bostonian for subway—to University Housing, to the "T," and now down Bay State Road, I stopped to rest. It was hot and humid and I was worn out by a day that began with packing in Fresno, California. Sitting on my suitcase, I scanned the addresses of the brownstones. I thought 92 Bay State Road would be at least a block closer. How much farther?

I heard a delightful, familiar voice, "Fado Potato!"

I was nicknamed Fado Potato last year at a Halloween party. In a costume made of stuffed beige garbage bags, I was a potato, and along with friends dressed as a tomato, carrot, and onion, with a bed sheet wrapped around us, we shuffled into the party and introduced our bowl of vegetable soup with a comedic song and dance. Each vegetable hopped out of the bowl and sang a verse to introduce themselves, and I sang "I'm Fado Potato and I'm looking for a spud!" The name stuck.

"Hey Mahz!," I called out loudly. I nicknamed Nancy Marsden "Mahz" because hailing from Massachusetts, the "r" sound is missing when pronouncing her last name. The nickname stuck.

If someone were to ask for Nancy or Donna at Boston University School of Theology, most would not know who they're talking about. We were both known by our nicknames.

A hot and humid August day, our hug to greet one another was brief.

Quickly, with the zeal of playing a great game of ping pong, our words bopped back and forth in delight.

"Good to see you!"

"You, too!"

"How was your summer?"

"Good!"

"How was yours?"

"Good, too."

"Let me help you with the suitcase," Mahz offered, and picked up the suitcase. "Good Lord, Fado, what do you have in here?

"You know, books, and everything."

"It weighs a ton."

"I know."

Walking together down the sidewalk, Mahz asked, "Have you been in the house yet?"

"No, just got here."

"Wait until you see it," she promised, unlocking both the outside and vestibule door to enter the brownstone.

The house smelled like fresh paint, furniture polish, and new carpet. Two brownstones had been merged into one, with a shared living room, eating area, and an extra large residential style kitchen on the first floor. Intricately carved mahogany railings lined two sets of stairs, one at each side of the house, leading to dormitory rooms above.

"Oh my goodness!" I gushed, taking in the accoutrements and heads and tails improvements over the building we lived in last year, the one that had housed twelve theology students for more than sixty years.

Together we hightailed it upstairs to the second floor landing with two large double rooms, one single room, and a bathroom. At home, in college, and during my first year of graduate school, I had always shared a room. Boston University School of Theology granted me a full tuition and living expenses scholarship, automatically renewed each year by maintaining an A minus grade point average, so with my work income I could afford a single room, finally.

Fitting the key into the vintage brass door knob, I opened the door to my room. Mahz and I peered inside and then stared stoically at one another. Clearly this room had been used in years past as a closet, just long, wide, and deep enough to fit a twin bed, desk, tall dresser, and aisle to walk sideways through. A few years later, University Housing converted the room for storage because it was not large enough to charge for a single.

Concealing our disappointment, Mahz and I commented on the positive.

"Fado, you've got your single room!"

Yay! Finally! Privacy.

"And it has a window that overlooks the street!" I added, feigning excitement. Last year the window of my double room faced the alley, and Mahz and I would crawl out the window onto the the fire escape, smoke cigarettes, and visit. The alley is home to rough stuff, including river rats, smelly garbage, drunken students, loud fights, and clandestine sex. A window overlooking the street is a vast improvement.

Opening the window, I pointed out another positive. "I love the cross breeze."

We sat down together on the twin bed, looked at one another, and I confessed the obvious, "It sure is small."

"You can always come downstairs and visit me," Mahz said.

"Sure thing."

At that moment, Mahz chose not to tell me about her room provided by her work as Resident Advisor. Last year, the RA room was a small single. In the new Theology House, it is an apartment with a living room, bedroom, kitchen, and bathroom.

I shut out of my mind and heart, the "too small" assessment. As if soiled laundry destined for the hamper, I recognized the smelliness of negative sentiment, and tossed it away to be cleaned. No use dwelling on what cannot be changed.

4: A Love Story

I got to know Hubert Ivery when he moved into the women's dormitory at Boston University by mistake. Hubert, a towering Black man, Baptist minister, and Southern gentleman is the last guy on earth who would move into the women's dormitory!

The new Theology House had a men's side and a women's side and shared the same street address and communal living areas on the ground floor. The room numbers painted on the dorm doors were not updated during the remodel. Hubert didn't know that. Mahz didn't know that. As Resident Advisor, Mahz mistakingly directed Hubert to the women's side and room next door to mine. For four days before the other students moved in, Mahz, Hubert, and I were alone in the rambling house. We toured a few sites in Boston, shared meals, watched TV, and hung out together. The three of us became solid friends.

There was quite a ruckus when a white woman assigned to the double room next door to mine discovered Hubert as her roommate. Mahz worked out the error. Hubert's computer slip from University Housing was correct, and so was the young woman's computer slip, which had the same room number on it. Hubert just needed to move into the men's dormitory, on the other side of the house.

Never had I considered it beyond-the-norm for me to have a man living next door to me in the dormitory. At UC Davis, I lived in a co-ed, door-by-door dormitory, but this liberal arrangement hadn't yet moved to Boston.

I'm glad Hubert initially moved into the women's dorm. I believe it to be a divinely appointed mistake.

Darn. I liked having Hubert as my neighbor. He is a gentle giant: easy-going, kind, and has a sense of humor that clicks with mine. He even fixed my light-up mirror!

When five women share one homestyle bathroom, those who are considerate do their make-up, blow drying, etcetera, in their own rooms. In the eighties curling irons and blow dryers were standard fare. When I received the light-up mirror as a graduation gift in high school, I wondered why I would need one. Makeup was not my thing, but I was appreciative of the gift. What I didn't know is how functional it would be in a dorm room: a mirror for the bedroom where all primping should be done. And, more important, it sat atop my chest of drawers and had an outlet on its front, doubling as an easy access extension cord for other electronic devices.

When it blew out one day, I prepared to go out and buy a replacement, an unexpected expense. I would have to spend my morning taking the "T"—short for the MBTA, of Metropolitan Bay Transit Association, or the subway— downtown and shop around. I had other things I'd rather be doing.

"Would you like me to take a look at it?" Hubert asked.

"Sure," I replied, a bit touched by his offer of help.

Hubert borrowed a screwdriver from a maintenance

worker and pulled the mirror apart, lining up the tiny little pieces of I-don't-know-what on the desk. He then put it back together, and voilà, my light-up mirror worked. I was super impressed. Hubert, I discovered, has a bachelor's degree in Electronic Engineering Technology and enjoys fixing or creating anything electronic.

A few months later, wearing my red plaid flannel nightgown worn smooth by years of washing, I sat in the community kitchen eating my breakfast quesadilla and drinking my cup of morning joe. The caffeine lubricated my eyelids heavy from sleep. The previous night I'd worked late as a cocktail waitress at a jazz bar in a five star hotel. That afternoon I would work as a personal assistant in the evangelism office on campus, striking a balance between the worldly ways of the bar and religion.

Hubert pulled out a chair and sat across from me. He was eating his standard fare: cornflakes with milk and a banana. I'd noticed that he ate cereal for most of his meals other than our community dinner. In our meal plan, about twenty students cook dinner and do dishes twice a month on weekdays. It's nice having dinner ready Monday through Friday. I'd noticed how well Hubert could cook and lay it all out. Two others had the opposite reputation. They fed our clan for less than five dollars with a soup of instant broth with floating pieces of lettuce and sinking beans. One week Hubert made chicken cacciatore with salad, vegetables, broccoli, french bread, and pie. Hubert, Mahz, and I seemed to have a similar value of hospitality. We might skimp on our own meals, but never the ones we provided for the community.

"Good morning," Hubert greeted me.

"Good morning to you," I said, just awake enough to speak.

Hubert smelled good, freshly showered with just a hint of scent, perhaps aftershave or cologne. He looked good, too, his hair and beard trimmed close, polo shirt and jeans pressed. He was quite the opposite of me. I had bed hair and my nightgown had tears along the shoulder seam and bottom ruffle—as long as nothing is showing that shouldn't, my comfy nightgown was functional and suited me just fine.

"Donna, I was wondering ..."

"Yeah?"

"I need to interview someone for a paper in my religious development class." He paused to gauge my reaction before going on. "Would you be available?"

"What kind of questions?" I asked.

"Like how your image of God has changed over the years and some of the experiences that have been significant in your religious development."

"Oh, sure, if we can find a good time," I said, tallying

my study, work, and class hours in my head. "How long of an interview?"

He could sense that my only hesitancy was fitting it into my tight schedule to coordinate with his work schedule. Three days a week he lived away as a resident counselor at a home for disabled adults.

"Only about forty-five minutes."

"How about tomorrow evening at eight o'clock?"

"That works for me," Hubert said. "I'll come to your room, if that's where you'd like to meet."

"Sounds great," I said as I cleared my plate, washed my frying pan and dishes, and took the stairs two at a time to throw on some clothes and get to class.

The forty-five minute interview for a paper evolved into a three-hour conversation in which both of us shared some of our religious development and experiences. I think that these are the moments in which I fell in love. What does a crass, loud, smoking, and drinking woman have in common with a quiet, courteous teetotaling man? What does a progressive United Methodist student working to change the church's antiquated position on gender parity and equality have to do with a Black Baptist pastor from the South? I, too, assumed probably not much. But I was so wrong.

We were both raised by strong, church-going families.

He, the eldest son of eight children to Eula and Leroy Ivery of Mount Pleasant, Alabama. Me, the second eldest daughter of four children to Don and Jean Fado of Fresno, California.

My dad is a United Methodist minister and my mother a singer. They met at the College of the Pacific in the fifties when he was the student body president and she had the lead in the opera. Mom has an amazing voice, a gift from the heavens, and was raised in Hollywood. Her mother taught piano and voice and her father provided for the family with a blue collar job. She was in a few movies, sang at the Hollywood Bowl, and was even on the cover of Colliers Magazine. She gave it all up to be a wife and mother.

Dad is a gifted preacher passionate about ministry, and stronger for the work because he has a partner in Mom. While at his first church in Fresno, California, a conservative valley town, he marched with Martin Luther King, Jr. While pastor at the Hanford United Methodist Church, a church of farmers, his ministry included advocacy for the farmworkers and Caesar Chavez. In the seventies he led the Wesley United Methodist Church in Fresno, California to be one of the two first "reconciling congregations" in our denomination nationwide to open its doors without condemnation to anyone, regardless of sexual orientation. Because he preached a strong biblical foundation relevant to the present day and comforted those who needed pastoral care, people of differing opinions were able to worship in one church together, and the churches grew.

4: A Love Story

Perhaps because of my parents, I'm not fazed by people disagreeing with how the scriptures speak to me and when a God of justice and healing leads me to prophetic work. Love can open our eyes to freedom and change. By definition, a prophet is always led by God beyond the status quo.

I'm proud to have been given the name, "Donna Jean," a junior for my parents, Don and Jean. They're both awesome people. What a great heritage.

I've always had an affinity for nature. Nana, or Grandma Fado, nicknamed me Ferdinand after the nature-loving bull of the children's book because I was the child lagging behind smelling the flowers. In the second grade, when I got my first pair of eyeglasses, in a contemporary cat's-eye style, I stared at the treetops, amazed by all of the individual leaves. In junior high school, backpacking with the church youth group, I felt the beauty of God's created world. There, for the first time, I fit in where I belonged, a wee piece in harmony with God's mysterious creation, one grain of sand on the beach, one drop of water in a mighty ocean. In the forest, God became not just the love of family, or what my parents taught me, or what my church expected me to believe. God became a spiritual presence, a palpable love that has the strength of roaring waters that can erode mountains, the softness of the downy fuzz on a baby chick, and a destiny and vision for my future that is as organic as growing up.

My adolescence was tough. By junior high I was almost my full adult height, five-foot-nine and a head taller than most girls and boys. I didn't wash my long brown hair or face often enough, had acne, crooked teeth, and usually crooked eyeglasses. Worse still, I followed a sugar-free diet for hypoglycemia, and saccharin gave me gas that would clear a room. My nickname in orchestra was "Deflato." I hid in books.

In youth group, I was taught that I am loved just as I am. With about twenty middle schoolers and a few youth counselors, we joined in social activities, dances, retreats, service projects, and backpacking trips. We also learned about the "God stuff," building blocks for how to love God, yourself, and your neighbor, which is the essence of Christianity. When Jesus was questioned about which is the greatest commandment, he said:

> 'Love the Lord your God with all your heart and with all your soul and with all your mind.' This is the first and greatest commandment. And the second is like it: 'Love your neighbor as yourself.'
>
> Matthew 22:37-39 (NIV)

Upon the spirit of Hubert Ivery I discovered a soft place where I could allow myself to fall, with laughter, delight, trust, and understanding. Both Hubert's and my religious values ran deeply and profoundly, those deep river currents coalesced and swept us up, up, and away to our first kiss.

We were both raised in families rooted in Christianity and love for one another. Ministers run in my family, including my great grandfather who was a hardshell Baptist traveling preacher. Hubert attended a small Baptist church filled with cousins and his preacher uncle, the only relative who shares his super-tall frame. Hubert remembers white folks with shotguns lining the Miami school where he was bused at the start of integration. The family safeguarded their children by sending four of the older ones to live with Grandma and Grandpa in the small rural community of Mount Andrew, Alabama. From age eight to eleven Hubert lived with his grandparents and three siblings in a Jim Walter "shell home." Jim Walter homes made it possible for low-income families to buy a house with no-down payment financing with proof of deed. Sharecroppers could finally get off the "massa's" land and buy their first home, but they didn't come with plumbing, so most folks used the bathroom for storage and built an outhouse. Before moving into the luxurious Jim Walter home sans plumbing, his grandparents lived in an uninsulated shack with dirt floors built for slaves.

As a young boy at the Center Ridge Baptist Church, Hubert sat on the mourners' bench, reserved for those who have yet to find the Lord, in front of the sanctuary where members would pray for their souls. He churned butter, peeled potatoes, snapped peas, worked the farm, and attended a one-room segregated schoolhouse. Neither Grandma or Grandpa could read, so the children read to them from the Bible. Grandma sang hymns while she worked, and Grandpa sang hymns on his way home from work, both of them dedicated to that "Ole' Time Religion." Grandma and Grandpa encouraged Hubert to spend time by himself "to get religion." Going out into the woods, Hubert had a profound spiritual awakening while sitting quietly by a trickling stream. The simple life, rich heritage and positive identity of African and African American spiritual traditions are rooted within Hubert's life force that is his religion.

I, too, was raised in a loving, church-bound family. Going to church, praying before meals, and learning about our faith was a given.

But following that kiss, we talked about how it was not the right time for us to date. I told him I was fickle, having a good time dating different guys for the first time in my life. We remained friends, but the sparks between us had ignited coals that slowly burned hotter.

By Christmas, three months later, I had grown bored with dating and sworn off guys. So many of the guys whom I had dated at Boston University were not marriage material, or they were going to be pastors. The heaviest work days of the year for ministers are the high holy days, with extra services, pastoral calls, and emergent needs of parishioners. I don't understand how clergy couples do it with young children, as both parents are locked-in at work during the school vacation times that coincide with Christmas and Easter. Called to be both a pastor and a mother, I crossed off my marriageable material list any man going into the pastoral ministry.

Hubert had already been a pastor, and was working on his doctorate to be a professor. When we returned to the Theology House in January we were drawn to one another and began to see each other romantically, though surreptitiously. Keeping our relationship on the down-low would help with the inevitable backlash of discrimination against interracial relationships.

One afternoon Hubert and I were studying together in my room, he at the desk, and me on the bed.

I looked up from my oh-so-dry church history book and said, "Hubert?"

"Yes?" Most of my friends would say, "yeah," but not Mr. Southern gentleman. He answered, "Yes."

"I think our relationship is getting pretty deep." Only three weeks of dating, and I was feeling a love surge to dive-in head first. I wanted to make sure the water was deep enough, otherwise I would need to find another pool.

Hubert paused to think.

I pressed on further to test the waters and quietly said, "I'm feeling a deep love for you."

"And I love you, too," Hubert confessed.

"I think it's time that we decide where this is going," I said, checking his reaction, and tentatively continued. "Uh..." I took a deep breath, braced myself, and dove-in, "if it's not going all the way we need to break it off so that we won't more-deeply hurt each another."

"Um hmm," Hubert agreed, the depths of his eyes drew me closer and didn't push me away.

Good. It's fine that I raised the issue.

"Let me go pray about it," Hubert offered in an intimate and sincere voice. He got up and left my dormitory room.

What the hell?

Being left alone isn't really the ideal climax to what I had read as a defining romantic moment. But really, Fado. You know Hubert. There isn't a more heartfelt and in-depth response than for him to go away and pray for awhile.

An hour and a half later I heard a knock at my door. It was Hubert.

"May I come in?" he asked.

"Sure."

Once the door was closed, he turned to me and simply said, "Will you marry me?"

"Yes!" I gushed, pushing myself up on tippy-toes and reaching my hands up and around his neck. We locked lips

4: A Love Story

in a passionate, hungry kiss.

Both sets of our parents were accepting of our starry-eyed love, and seemed happy to see us walking on clouds.

Visiting his family in Miami, Florida, Hubert showed his parents a picture of me. I am fair-skinned, about as white as they come, always very pale or noticeably sunburned. His mother reacted earnestly, "She shooor is white!"

Visiting my family in Fresno, California, I showed my parents a picture of Hubert. Within the broad range of African American skin tones, Hubert is beautifully, deeply, dark-skinned. My dad responded by stating the obvious, "He sure is black!"

So many ways the same, and yet so different.

Six months later we announced our engagement. Like instantaneous ripples spreading upon the water when a stone is dropped, a discernible circle of currents rolled right along as normal things do. At Macy's picking out our china pattern for the wedding registry, the clerk repeatedly and purposefully overlooked our presence to serve other customers. At the convenience store, only when I was with Hubert standing in line, I was waited on last at the cash register, no matter how long the line. In the Boston University School of Theology Dean's Office I endured a conversation about the marriage being a strategic ploy for my advancement in the institutional church. Say what? And, of course, there was more.

Especially in the 1980's, most graduate students in

theology had an unwavering affinity for church history, the holy scriptures, and church tradition. Particularly in that milieu a Progressive Baptist marrying a United Methodist, an African American man marrying a Caucasian woman, was breaking tradition and hard to swallow. Between me and too many classmates, I felt a discernible shift within our intercommunication. Sure, surface words remained cordial, but their eyes communicated distrust rather than interest, their energies communicated barriers rather than openness.

I prayed about these new experiences of my own community reacting to me with suspicion. I felt God's answer with a misting of warmth on my heart.

God said, "Yeah?"

As Hubert and I united in our love for one another, the Spirit present in our relationship emboldened me to stand firm and let those who press conformity and normality to be repelled. Falseness flaked off like shedding dead skin.

We married two years later, just after my graduation from Boston University School of Theology and before my first full-time pastoral job in California. The day after the late May commencement, Mahz, Hubert, and I drove cross-country in our Ford Escort with all of our belongings in a rooftop carrier. On June 7, 1986, Hubert and I were married in Fresno, California, at my home church, Wesley United Methodist Church. Our wedding party consisted of Mahz, a Roman Catholic; the best man, Rozelle, a Church of God in Christ minister; the groom, a Progressive Baptist minister; and the bride, a United Methodist soon-to-be ordained minister. My dad, a United Methodist minister, and the Reverend Dr. Chester Williams, a Christian Methodist Episcopal minister, officiated. That's five ministers from different denominations in a wedding party of seven.

For our honeymoon we stayed at a friend's condominium at Bass Lake, close to Yosemite National Park. But, we had to cut our four-day honeymoon in half for me to interview for the position of associate pastor at the Asbury United Methodist Church in Livermore.

When the bishop's cabinet, or supervisory clergy who work with the bishop, calls a United Methodist minister to interview for a pastoral position, it's the time to drop everything and GO. In the United Methodist Church, clergy are "appointed" to a church by a bishop who oversees a "conference," a geographical area covering usually a state or two. At the beginning of American Methodism, at the Christmas Conference in 1784, two bishops were ordained to supervise and send out preachers on horseback to our young nation's frontier. Ever since, at an annual conference, the bishop appoints his/her traveling preachers to an area. In yesteryears the appointment could have been for a circuit rider to cover the state of Montana, and today it may be for a pastor to serve one church, or three churches. The church provides housing as pastors can come and go quickly, like those serving and living on military bases. All of the conference clergy move the same week of the year, flip-flopping homes, to begin their appointments on July 1st. Becoming a clergy member of the conference typically requires a three-year professional degree/ the Master of Divinity, and five-to-ten years of supervision and probation. As a United Methodist minister, I agree to "go where the bishop sends me."

The personnel committee of a United Methodist Church interviews one person, the bishop's choice. If either the church or prospective pastor sees a major reason why the match won't work, only then will there be a possibility of a second candidate, at the discretion of the bishop. For many churches in the 1980s, the prospect of having a female pastor was uncomfortable. But in the California-Nevada Annual Conference of the United Methodist Church, "We don't want a woman minister," was not an acceptable protest, and my bishop would often appoint the woman anyway. The United Methodist system has been at the forefront of clergywomen employment in a male-dominated field.

With an electric air of excitement Hubert and I arrived in Livermore an hour before the interview to check out what kind of city we would be living in. Nestled in the Livermore Valley about an hour east of the San Francisco Bay, the area presented historic vineyards, a quaint town, family farms, housing developments, and the Lawrence Livermore Lab, the place of nuclear research and highly educated employees. Tracing our fingers along the paper map, we checked out the church. On a ten-acre plot of dry wild grass, a cluster of small nondescript church buildings sat behind a green grass front yard with an easy-to-miss Asbury United Methodist Church sign.

At my interview, the committee of a dozen or so folks fanned my excitement for ministry. The church is real people, a community of faith, not a building. Asbury is bursting at the seams. My job description included education, youth ministry, preaching, pastoral care, and working with the senior pastor, Richard Ernst. Hubert came with me to the interview, and my senses were on high alert to discern this 98% white church's reaction to my new husband. They were gracious and welcoming. They would find and rent an apartment or condo for us to call home. As newlyweds we owned a mug collection, desk, electric typewriter, Kaypro computer, Ford Escort, and yet-to-be-opened wedding gifts. A personnel committee member offered, "We'd love to get you set up in your first home. We have experience setting up homes for refugees." The entirety of our household furniture was donated.

The next week we attended the Session of the California-Nevada Annual Conference in Reno, Nevada, where I was ordained deacon in a grand worship service with all the pomp and circumstance that United Methodists can muster. A few days later we moved to Livermore. On July 1, 1986, I began work.

All in six weeks: graduation in Boston, marriage in Fresno, ordination in Reno, and work in Livermore. What a whirlwind! Everything flew into place seamlessly, which is the way things can happen when we align ourselves with God's desire for us. With the Holy Spirit in our sails, Hubert and I were in for the ride of our lives.

While taking courses for his Ph.D. in San Francisco, Hubert worked many jobs such as substitute teaching, Radio Shack sales, and overnight guard on a Christmas tree lot. With one car and bicycles, we both were able to get around town. The often requested substitute teacher, Hubert had a reputation for being able to manage the notoriously difficult middle school classes. Once he came home in a dash from substitute teaching to change into his sweats and tennis shoes and to pick up his college NAIA championship ring. He had told the rowdy boys, "If you're good in class, I'll show you my ring and play basketball with you after school."

After pastoring almost two years, I submitted to the Bishop's cabinet my appointment request to "either" stay or move to another church. I was ready to be a solo pastor, but enjoyed serving Asbury. Being willing to move or stay gives the bishop flexibility to find a church that is a good match. I asked that my next appointment be to a church in an ethnically diverse community. I was still getting used to those who reacted to our interracial marriage with derisive stares and snarky comments, though of course, there were those who welcomed us with open hearts and arms.

And then on a late afternoon in April, Hubert arrived home and appeared to be pretty shook-up. I was cooking dinner. He took a seat at the nearby dining table.

Usually Hubert emitted a calm, deep river energy, but in that moment it felt to me that his energy was like ocean undulating and choppy surface waters. "What's goin' on?" I asked.

"I was walking downtown, in front of the post office," Hubert calmly said, and then paused.

Uh oh. He had my complete attention. I looked him in the eye and waited.

"And this pickup truck ran up onto the sidewalk and pretended to try to hit me."

My mouth gaped open, an icy waterfall pelted down upon me, and I tried to quell my shivering.

Hubert attempted to minimize the danger, maybe for me, but I think also for himself. "They were probably just having fun, joking around," he said.

A long silence. I wish he would say more. Now was about him and not me.

"They yelled something at me."

"Something derogatory?" I asked, even though I was thinking the "n" word, a word which I would not utter in my home.

Hubert nodded.

"The "n" word?"

He nodded again.

"Rednecks?" The word rarely escaped my mouth, but in my own mind it meant country garb and music drowning in racial intolerance.

"I guess you could say that. A couple of young guys."

"High school?"

"No, older."

We held each other close.

The next day, I called my District Superintendent and asked to be moved as soon as possible. It was late in the appointment process to request a change, but it just so happened that a pastor at another church also had a late-notice-move-request from someone planning to attend school. Within the week the call came for me to interview for the position of pastor at the Wesley United Methodist Church in Hayward, a more diverse community in the San Francisco Bay Area.

The church was such a joy, so open to creativity in worship, able to try new things, and filled with loving people of different ages and cultures. While pastoring the church in Hayward for five years, Hubert and I were blessed by the births of two daughters.

Hubert and Donna Wedding Day, June 1986

We named our first baby Aisha Lucile, with grounding in both of our cultures. Aisha, which rhymes with Alicia, is a Swahili name which means "full of life," and Lucile is my Nana's name.

When Aisha was a year old, we gathered for a Fado family reunion for the celebration of my grandparents' 70th wedding anniversary. There, one relative asked, "Where in the world did you find a name like Aisha?" She had not heard the name before.

The next month when we gathered for Hubert's family reunion down South, one relative asked, "Where in the world did you find a name like Lucile?" She had not heard the name before.

Hubert completed his Ph.D. coursework and worked as Chaplain at a residential treatment home for troubled youth, the Fred Finch Youth Center, in Oakland. He decided at that time to become a United Methodist minister.

We named our second baby Imani Lee, again with grounding in both of our cultures. Imani, pronounced EE-mah-knee, is a Swahili name that means "faith," and Lee is an Ivery family name.

Two weeks after giving birth to Imani, I received a surprise phone call from the Bishop's cabinet, asking me to interview for the position of Senior Pastor at the Madera United Methodist Church in the San Joaquin Valley of California. Hubert was asked to interview for the positions of part-time associate pastor at the same church as well as part-time pastor at a small African American United Methodist Church, the St. Mark's United Methodist Church in nearby Fresno. My maternity leave was joyfully speckled by hiking

4: A Love Story

Bryce Canyon in Utah, finding a place to live in Madera, and packing up the house. In a course of three months, we had added a second baby to our family, bought our first home, moved, and started new jobs. Whoosh! Another ride as when our sails once again catch the movement of the Holy Spirit!

Hubert and I conscientiously nurture a relationship and family that embodies cultural and religious diversity. The work of Florence Kluckholn in the area of culture and values orientation has helped us to identify how we differ without breeding contempt, the death knell for a relationship. How do we best think about time? Hubert's culture draws from the past and history to prepare for the future. My culture looks to the future with sacrifice and goal setting. It's not that one is better than the other, we are different.

Our marriage is a learning lab for what veins of cultural assumptions, learning styles, and habits are at play both above and below the surface. It's like baking a cake with the Holy Spirit as the heat of the oven, balancing the amounts of diverse ingredients. In my interracial, cross-cultural marriage, I am not repeating the recipe with which I was raised, and neither is Hubert. It is not that our ingredients are bad. He is accustomed to adding real butter, brown sugar, and three eggs to flour. I am accustomed to adding white shortening, powdered sugar, and two eggs to flour. I show up to an appointment five minutes early, and he within fifteen minutes. I prefer to drive tried and true main streets, and Hubert likes to explore back streets. I build plans from the specific to general, and he from the general to specific. I listen first to words, and he first intuits the context, including tone of voice and the feelings beneath the words. He sweeps and cleans the floors first, I declutter and clean off the counters first. I choose not to wear or buy clothes that need ironing because ironing is a waste of my time. He irons his clothes, whether or not they need it, every morning. I am extroverted, he is introverted. I start a project with a neat desk, and he with a messy desk, so our experiment of sharing an office didn't work. He is not thrown by racism, because he knows it well and has been raised within a culture of defiance. I am thrown by racism because growing up white, generally I expect institutions and people to be fair and hard work to be rewarded.

How on earth does a marriage with such diversity work?

We have a strong bond of love beneath it all, an elaborate musculature that works together beneath a skin of differences. We are graced by a spiritual camaraderie, and our natural inclination to be truly helpful to one another. More important, there is an additional energy, beyond who we are, whom we know as God, who helps to make our relationship work.

This deep well of spirituality would sustain us through the shattering and desert dwelling of brain injury.

5: Desert Dwelling

January 26 -December 1994

BECAUSE I DID NOT PASS OUT upon impact and could answer questions intelligibly, a CT Scan to check for bleeding in the brain was not ordered. In 1994 emergency medicine protocol was that a patient must lose consciousness to have a brain injury. Nowadays the protocol has changed. At Barton Memorial Hospital an X-ray confirmed that my neck was not broken. In only a few hours I was released with a cervical collar for whiplash and told to watch for signs of a concussion. If I were to develop nausea, confusion, headache, or dizziness, I should go to Emergency. And, of course, I should follow up with my personal physician as soon as I get home.

Back at the cabin, I lie down, put ice packs on my neck, and try not to think about how to clean the cabin, pack up, and leave the next morning. I have skipped dinner, and my stomach is rumbling. A lactating mom needs healthy food calories regularly and often. I am fixated on getting dinner.

"Hubert, I'm hungry."

"I don't think we have any food in the house. What do you want me to get for you?"

"Go back to the restaurant."

"Donna," Hubert says in a soft but unwavering voice that lays down the law, "I'm not going back there."

"Why not?"

"I'm not doing it."

"Then find me something, please," I say, resigning myself to eating whatever he can bring me.

Hubert goes to a nearby restaurant, The Swiss Lakewood Restaurant, a woodsy place we had noticed driving around Lake Tahoe. He brings me a beef mushroom stroganoff dinner that is oddly the most delicious meal I have ever eaten. When I remember that night, I taste that dinner again. I think about it, and my mouth waters.

Leaving the cabin the next morning, I grow headachy and nauseated while riding down the curvy mountain roads. I chalk it up to getting carsick. Two hours from Lake Tahoe, we stop in Sacramento for a meal at my Mom and Dad's before continuing the three-hour drive home to Madera. Once in Sacramento I feel too sick to ride any longer, so we get two hotel rooms. Paying for a hotel instead of riding in the car for three hours is something definitely out of the norm for me.

Hubert tells me I should go to Emergency. I refuse. Sitting for hours in the ER waiting room is beyond my ability. My understanding is foggy, my head hurts, and I feel like I am going to vomit. All I want to do is to get home to see my own doctor.

Two days later, on Monday, I see my personal physician at Kaiser. She tells me that I have a concussion, should take it easy, and can take some pain medicine. My concussion, gradually more apparent each day, is at its worst five days after my injury, with stabbing pain at the left side and back of my head where I was struck by the glass. Two weeks later I am diagnosed as having "post-concussive syndrome," meaning a concussion that for some reason hasn't gone away. At the time, Kaiser protocol is not to order a CT Scan for concussions until three weeks after injury because most of them resolve and the expensive test is unnecessary. Five weeks after my injury I have a CT Scan. It is normal.

These are the years before the National Brain Injury Association set out to educate the medical establishment that a patient can have a serious brain injury without losing consciousness. Misdiagnosis and postponed or missed rehabilitation are the downside of having an injury that is on the cusp of new discoveries in medicine.

The over two-hundred-pound plate glass partition didn't shatter when it landed on me, but parts of my brain did. All of a sudden "doing" has become a strenuous activity, as has thinking, writing, remembering, reading, grabbing, speaking, and walking. Hubert finds full-time daycare for the baby and immediately becomes primary caregiver for the children— and for me.

On the back of my head, a walnut-sized lump enshrines the first walloping strike of that plate glass partition, memorializing what is no longer: an active life. At age thirty-two I go from exercising three times a week doing step aerobics at the athletic club, serving as senior pastor of a multi-staffed church, and reading at least a book a week for sermons, to being a woman wrapped in a sodden blanket of chronic pain, unable to read a short magazine article, unable to work, worn out by taking a shower or expending a full day of energy by sitting in a recliner pulled out to the driveway to watch her four year old rollerskate for twenty minutes.

My body has sounded an alarm, a knife stabbing repeatedly into my head just above my left ear, to protest the onslaught of the second strike of that partition. In the ensuing years, the alarm will not turn off, and I will be left with the constant companion of chronic pain.

My personal physician who, blessedly, listens closely and is able to see the undeniable difference of me pre and post injury, announces, "We don't know how long your post-concussive syndrome will last. We just need to wait and see."

I discover my HMO is notoriously good at waiting: a five-week wait for a CT Scan of the brain, four month wait for an MRI, five month wait for a referral to see a neurologist.

5: Desert Dwelling

My post-concussive syndrome is a square peg trying to fit into the round hole of the healthcare system.

Three months after my injury an Occupational Medicine doctor evaluating my condition notes that panic is the cause of my problems, including my left side weakness and memory loss. He writes "hysteria" as my diagnosis. The term hysteria dates back to the 5th century BC when Hippocrates postulated that female madness is linked to the uterus, *hystera*, a pseudoscience diagnosis that wasn't dropped by the American Psychiatric Association until the 1950s. It's really creepy that I take him seriously. Swimming through the unsure footing of my mind, memory, and body, I don't have the mental bandwidth to question his authority and grasp at his diagnosis as if it is a life raft on troubled water.

I spend the first year following my brain injury doing exactly what the doctors order, expecting to get back to normal. That doesn't happen.

Within the inner landscape of my mind I dwell in a desert land of not knowing. Not knowing my phone number to access my account at the video store. Not knowing last names so that my address book or church directory were no longer usable. Not knowing the name of my nephew in a family gathering. Not knowing the last number when counting, so following a recipe is impossible. Cooking rice in the microwave, involving counting two cups of rice and four cups of water should be simple, but the number of times I smoke up the house by burning that simple dish is telling. Not knowing a word, so that word finding feels like searching the University library stacks for a single book. Not knowing how to speak clearly, because enunciating consonants feel like speaking with a mouth full of peanut butter. Not knowing where a glass is located in reference to my body, so that I knock it over when reaching for it.

The church community of the Madera United Methodist Church are heroes and she-roes of support. For three months they deliver homemade dinners to us. For the first year church members drive me to doctors' appointments and three times a week to physical therapy sessions. They pray for my healing. They are gentle, caring, and supportive, an expansive blessing.

Three months after my injury I begin to attend worship again at church. I enjoy worship, the songs, the prayers, the readings, the children, the people who care so deeply, and most of all the detectable energy swell when a group of people focus their hearts and minds together in prayer. Say, for instance that one person meditates on peace. When three people together meditate on peace there is a spilling over, an added measure of peace. This is the profound gift of communal worship.

During worship service, Aisha goes to Sunday School class for four-year-olds and Imani to the nursery. Hubert and the retired pastor filling in for me lead the service. I sit in the way back of the pew-lined sanctuary, so that I can slip out halfway through the one-hour service when my headache becomes unmanageable. While seated my head feels progressively heavier, so much so that I can no longer hold it up. Then the words and music blur. I stay as long as I can, and then walk slowly, in an awkward waddle, to Hubert's office where I crawl onto a floor mat and cuddle beneath a comforter. With my eyes closed and body stilled, every breath serves to restore me. An hour later I walk out of the office to briefly visit folks congregated in the social hall for refreshments, then walk to the car to go home with Hubert and the girls. Going to worship is a time of huge exertion. I spend the rest of the day, as well as the next day, in bed.

Hubert and Aisha bring lunch and dinner to me in bed. For brief interludes I watch *Barney* and *Spot the Dog* with Aisha. At Imani's nap time Hubert brings her to me, and she snuggles on top of me, her sweet cheek against my breasts, the rise and fall of my chest lulling her to sleep. I hold her there as she sleeps, fostering our bond. With my concussion, the back and forth sway of the rocking chair immediately brings on intense nausea, so I have had to give up my cherished ritual of rocking Imani to sleep. Three days after the accident, my doctor prescribed Ibuprofen for my headache and ordered that I stop nursing Imani. To abruptly give up rocking and nursing Imani weighs heavily on me, as if a millstone tied around my mother's heart has dropped into the sea. That sinking feeling reminds me of one of Jesus' teachings.

It would be better for you if a millstone were hung around your neck and you were thrown into the sea than for you to cause one of these little ones to stumble.
                              Luke 17:2 (NRSV)

Fortunately, I had developed a relationship with a good therapist in the five months before my injury. Given my long silent pauses and how difficult it is me to speak after a ride in a moving car to Fresno, it would now be virtually impossible for me to get to know a therapist. To those who haven't known me pre-injury, I present as normal, perhaps as a woman who merely twisted her ankle and needed a cane. My therapist can see the dramatic difference in me pre- and post-injury, and that alone is a touchstone of truth.

With my HMO diagnoses of panic and hysteria as the cause of my problems and therefore no rehabilitation, as well as a wait of five months post-injury for me to see a neurologist, Hubert and I decide to opt for an evaluation by a neurologist outside of the Kaiser system—a big bill, but a necessary safeguard.

"I could do more for someone with a gunshot wound to the head than for you," the neurologist explains, "at least then

I could do surgery and repair the localized area of the gunshot. When you were hit on the back of the head, your brain slapped against the front of your skull, and when you were hit on the left side of your head, the brain slapped against the right side of your skull. Because of this 'contra coup' concussion, you have injuries in every quadrant of your brain. I didn't go to medical school to work with patients I cannot help."

If my brain were a china plate, broken into five pieces, the surgeon could carefully glue it back together. But my brain had dropped and smashed to smithereens. Too many tiny pieces to fix. And, because I don't have seizures —*thank God*— I don't need medicine. No surgery. No medicine. My brain injury has nothing that the specialty of neurology is trained to handle.

I am silent and look to the floor, because the floor in this moment is the only surface strong enough and wide enough and willing enough to hold up the shattering of my brain, because looking at the floor I can hide the tears welling up in my eyes. "But my problems are neurological?" I ask.

"Yes," she answers, "but I cannot help you."

At least I now know that my problems are neurological. It has been four months since my injury, and finally I am seeing an expert in the medical field. For the length of the long ride home, Hubert and I maintain silence, a padded cell to contain my emotional turmoil, which struggles to unleash.

Barely containing myself, I clamp my jaw shut, push back the lump in my throat, and wipe away the stray tears escaping from my closed eyelids. I am reeling from the neurologist's blunt assessment. It slams the door shut on medical help for me. *My problem is neurological, but no neurologist can help me.*

Back at home, Hubert helps me to walk down the long hallway to our bedroom, tucks me into bed, and brings me a glass of water. The moment he closes the door and I am alone, the dam breaks and I break down.

The waters of my tears slowly erode the lump in my throat and the pit in my stomach. The Spirit works through my tears to wash any encumbrance muddying my soul self, and I reconcile myself to the inability of medical knowledge to heal me. In the past four months I have done everything possible to do what the doctors ordered. I have brought typed notes to each appointment because after riding in the car I cannot speak very well or think very clearly though I want to communicate most effectively and use the time most efficiently. I have dedicated myself to following through with my esteemed doctors recommendations more than I had dedicated myself to academics, but my work at school was rewarded with scholarships and honors while my work to follow medical directions has been rewarded with a closed door.

A whisper within beckons to me. *The spiritual door has not shut on you.*

5: Desert Dwelling

My own certainty of knowing has slipped. My doctors' seeming omniscience has been called into question. Where is the authority for my healing. Medicine? A helpful science with expertise upon which I might lean, medicine does not have all the answers. Where will I find the authority, the source of answers and directions, so that I can find healing? Me? I *should* be able to figure out how to improve my health, but my thinking and remembering have been compromised. I cannot even count on me.

I am in a centrifuge, its spinning peeling away all that I have counted on, like medical fixes, a pain-free body, and dependable cognition. Oh ... so ... dizzy ... I can't keep it together anymore. I am too exhausted to cry, to stress, to pray, to care anymore. My fall into the centrifuge of injury shatters and peels away the shells of pretense. The yolk of who I am at my center spills out, slimy and unstructured.

Who I am soaks into the ground beneath, absorbing who I am. It is the *Ground of Being. It is God.* Twentieth century theologian, Paul Tillich, coined the phrase, *ground of being*, a name for God.

God is called the 'ground of being' because God is the answer to the ontological threat of non-being.

Paul Tillich
Systematic Theology, Volume I

The essence, the love of God, the Great I Am, the *Ground of Being* saves me as I crack wide open.

For the first time since the accident, I sleep deeply and peacefully. Awakened by the stabbing pain on the left side of my head, I take a pill for pain and soon drift off into blessed sleep again. Unhinged, I barely move from bed for a few days.

My denial, a necessary protective egg shell, has broken open prematurely. When I awaken from my flattened state, my consciousness has shifted. By faith, I have fallen not into the unknown; I have fallen upon God. God alone holds the ultimate authority for my healing. What is authority anyway? The word, authority, means the one to whom we look to and lean upon as master, leader, and author. No longer will I look to my mind or medicine for all the answers in my quest for healing. I will look to God who will lead me to the ways of healing, including the ways of self-help, medicine, and more. God is the *Author of my Soul*, the *Ground of Being*, the *Artist* who created me. Who better to lead me through the unknown?

Before the shift in my consciousness, I would awaken with plans to pursue medical treatment. I would awaken to a maelstrom of what I needed to do, but was unable to do. This morning, I have awakened to a heart, my heart, filled with thanksgiving and praise.

5: Desert Dwelling

Yea, I shall joyfully sing of Your lovingkindness in the morning, for You have been my stronghold and a refuge in the day of my distress.

Psalm 59:16b (AMP)

By odd coincidences and what I know to be answered prayer, within the next six months I am under the care of three medical professionals who worked together in the "early years" on mild traumatic brain injury: a neuropsychologist, a physiatrist, and an opthalmologist. While the HMO ophthalmologist finds nothing wrong with my eyes, the out-of-network ophthalmologist who understands brain injury finds seventeen things wrong with my eye-brain connection, including double vision, the inability to track motion, and eyes jerking when panning horizontally or vertically. All of these bring on nausea. The Physical Medicine and Rehabilitation doctor, or physiatrist, changes my diagnosis from post-concussive syndrome to mild traumatic brain injury (later called moderate brain injury). It has always seemed a misnomer that a "mild traumatic brain injury" could be a disabling condition, but considering that a major brain injury is coma, it's understandable. The continuum of major to moderate to mild brain injury is such a broad span. All not covered by my HMO insurance, these traumatic brain injury specialists are far too familiar with the frustration of delayed diagnosis. They assign rehabilitation exercises.

Sleep, Pray, Heal

The physiatrist prescribes cognitive exercises such as watching a TV program with Hubert and having him quiz me during commercials on what I have just seen and heard, playing Nintendo for eye/hand coordination, and keeping to a strict schedule of lying down for an hour for every hour up. This gentle retraining of the brain is quite the opposite of what I had been doing. My natural inclination is to work hard and push my limits to build stamina, a philosophy akin to lifting weights, but when I work on cleaning one room with the help of a grabber/reaching tool, I end up in bed for two days. When I go to water rehab exercises in the pool, as recommended by my primary care physician, my legs feel like cement, and I can't speak for the rest of the day. My physiatrist flips my healing axiom upside down. "The brain must rest to heal," he insists. "Overdoing can bring on seizures and increase pain." By keeping pain levels lower with rest, less narcotic pain medication is necessary. By lying down so frequently throughout the day, I actually have more up hours and rehab the brain. Playing with and enjoying my girls is rehab for brain injury. *Easy does it*.

The ophthalmologist prescribes eye exercises and prism eyeglasses for double vision. Holding a pencil at arm's length in front of me, I work to pull the two images of the pencil into one image, though doing this twice puts me under the table with nausea and increased headaches. Sitting at the table in the backyard, I work to pull the two images of a tree

78

together into one. Another exercise is to keep my head still and pan my eyes to the right and left, but doing this, my eyes are so jerky, I get seasick. Like my physiatrist, the ophthalmologist warns me that the brain must rest to heal and not to overdo.

PART II: PAINTING PRAYERS

When through the deep waters I call thee to go,
the rivers of woe shall not thee overflow;
for I will be with thee, thy troubles to bless,
and sanctify to thee thy deepest distress.

When through fiery trials thy pathways shall lie,
my grace, all sufficient, shall be thy supply;
the flame shall not hurt thee; I only design
thy dross to consume, and thy gold to refine.

John Rippon, 1787
How Firm a Foundation

6: Too Deep for Words
December 1994

PROPPED ON THE EASEL IN FRONT OF ME, the blank canvas board is formidable. Painting a picture of my pain is most definitely not the top of my list, or even on the list of what I would like to do. My therapist gave me this assignment. I pay good money for her guidance to help move me through the emotional sludge of injury, so I need to follow through and express what I'm experiencing. Generally when I meet with her, the motion of the car ride has spun my focus and I barely speak, long periods of silence a moat between us. Art will be a substitute for inaccessible words.

What makes you think you can do this, Fado?

I had enjoyed taking decorative painting lessons as a youth, duplicating the teacher's fruit or flower by color-blending recipes and stroke-by-stroke direction. Firmly planted in my psyche are the words of a visiting art professor at the University of California at Davis. "I don't think you have the talent to be an art major." The one art class at UC Davis and the ominous words of the professor put the kibosh on my desire to paint, and I packed away my brushes. The PBS painting show, *Bob Ross's Joy of Painting*, encouraged me otherwise. Since my head injury I haven't been able to tolerate many sitcoms or dramas because any consternation or surprises or violence or fast talking is too much for my already overwhelmed and slow-paced brain. Bob Ross speaks calmly, slowly, velvety, and incorporates stories of joy—like meeting a squirrel, or a sunset, or leaves on a tree. *Bob Ross says I can do this.*

I close my eyes, take a deep breath, and pray, *God help me do this.* I hear God's answer: flutter butterfly kisses on the inside of my forehead. *I have already helped you to do this.*

One of my favorite things to do in the pastoral ministry, and what I poured so much of myself into, was preaching. When I couldn't be in the pulpit on Easter Sunday, the highest holy day of the Christian year, I went through preaching withdrawal. A clergy sister had suggested to me that in this season of my healing, perhaps God is calling me to an alternate ministry, the same theme studied this year by the United Methodist Women, to *Make Plain the Vision.* In the Hebrew scriptures, God tells the prophet, Habakkuk, to sit in the tower and make plain the vision, to put on tablets everything he sees in the unknown territory so that a runner can read it, and that the work will be used at a later, appointed time.

> *I will take my stand to watch,*
> *and station myself on the tower,*
> *and look forth to see what he will say to me,*
> *and what I will answer concerning my complaint.*

Sleep, Pray, Heal

And the Lord answered me:
'Write the vision;
make it plain upon tablets,
so he may run who reads it.'

For still the vision awaits its time;
it hastens to the end—it will not lie.
If it seem slow, wait for it;
it will surely come, it will not delay

Habakkuk 2:1-3 (RSV)

Words are undependable for me—wrong words, missing words, not finding words—and are certainly not legible to someone jogging by. A picture is worth a thousand words, and can be quickly seen by a runner. Painting a picture of what I am experiencing in this uncharted wilderness of head injury resembles the prophet Habakkuk writing on tablets whatever he sees from his towering post, *so that a runner can read it.* In the last six months there hasn't been a week that this scripture didn't come to my mind. I wonder how it may be possible for me to paint again. I don't have the money to buy expensive tubes of oil paints or Bob Ross-size canvasses at twenty to seventy-five dollars a pop. We are in dire financial straits.

Hubert's part-time pastorate at the small Black Church in Fresno has been adjusted to quarter-time and the Bishop correctly yoked it with a nearby small church that concurrently reduced their pastoral time. Thus Hubert's work and income has gone from full time to part time. My disability pension from the United Methodist Church calculates a living wage by the combination of Social Security Disability and the pension. But it routinely takes over a year to get Social Security Disability. In addition to our salary being reduced by half we must now pay for our own health insurance. Our income has been cut in half and I haven't yet received Social Security Disability.

After the five month long ordeal of completing the Social Security Disability application, everything falls into place, like cards stacked in a deck to play.

- My brother's wife, an artist and expectant mother, decides to give away her oil paints because of their toxicity around her baby. A shoe box filled with expensive paints arrives in the mail.
- A family from the church owns a lumber yard and delivers twenty-two by twenty-eight inch masonite panels to my home for one dollar each.
- Hubert gives me an easel and Bob Ross starter set for Christmas.
- My therapist gives me the assignment to paint a picture of my pain.

After more than six months of discerning whether this was God's call to me to paint the truth of what I am experiencing in this frontier of brain injury — *whoosh*—God has confirmed my calling in a whirling shuffle of pieces that I have previously strained to pick up one by one.

Yes, Lord, you have helped me to do this. Please lead me now. It doesn't need to be artistic, just true.

My pain feels like it would be brick red, like the dried blood of a horrific accident, with accents of dead blue, harrowing blood and death courting my days and hours. I hastily squeeze out big slugs of Indian Red, Prussian Blue, and Titanium White paint.

With a two-inch brush I quickly lay down over the entire board a thinned-down background of Indian Red. Pain covers the totality of myself and the height of the sky with no breaks in the atmosphere. Along both vertical edges of the board I build with a palette knife two tall mountains with protruding spikes to illustrate pinching and stabbing pain. Both mountains jut out as cliffs with a long drop to the valley below which are also filled with dagger ends. If I were perched on the top, looking miles down below, my stomach would drop, and if I were in the dangerous ravine below, I wouldn't know how to escape. My lurching stomach and panic when finding no way out is part of pain's affliction. With a sash brush I dab on dark blue, like dark clouds, the blurred indistinguishable weight of a storm, yet another layer of pain.

Pain, oil on canvas board, 22×28, 1995

Sleep, Pray, Heal

With the back of my hand I wipe away my tears and the snot running from my nose. I hadn't realized I was crying during my ten-minute sprint of painting. It's so depressing that I know so damn intimately the ugly image before me.

The finished painting is sickening. I put it in my garage to dry. But oil paints don't dry in the damp of winter, so I have to move it inside. I put it behind closed doors in the living room. I hate seeing it. I move through what Elisabeth Kübler Ross describes as the stages of loss, and the painting moves through the house: from denial(the garage) to depression(the living room) to bargaining(the family room). Finally when I reach acceptance—no, that's not right; I've never accepted it. I guess it was the stage of anger—I hang it in my bedroom. When I lie down with excruciating headaches, I talk to the painting of my pain. I literally talk to it aloud and say, "You don't look as bad as you feel."

Pain

Deep pain.
Sharp pain.
Muddled pain taking over the sky.
No way to escape.
Seeing pain.
Sharing pain.
Self recovered within pain's grasp.

—Donna Fado Ivery, December 1994

7: Uncovering
January 1995

ONE YEAR AFTER MY HEAD INJURY, during the preponderance of hours lying in bed, a question continues to rise to the surface of my mind like a lapping tide. *What happened to me when the glass fell? O God, what the hell happened to me?*

As my therapist suggested, I decide to ask the question in a painting. *How do I do that? I don't know. Holy Spirit, lead me.*

Digging through my purse, I notice an old compact mirror with a cracked black plastic backing and an idea pops into my mind. I can paint the question, *What happened to me when the glass fell?* Tossing the compact into the laundry basket, I save steps by waiting until the laundry basket is full of diapers to hang out to dry on the line in the backyard. I throw the mirror onto the cement patio. *Nothing happens.* I try again, like throwing a fastball pitch, and *voilà* the mirror shatters.

Seated at the dining room table I look at myself in the mirrored wall and sketch with oil pastels a self portrait on newsprint. Following the pattern of the shattered mirror compact, I cut my self portrait out in the same pieces. Spacing apart the broken mirror pieces of my picture, I glue them onto a solid black twenty-two by twenty-eight inch masonite panel.

Finally! What is invisible is made visible. This is what happens when glass falls.

Missing connectors in my brain seem to have dismantled my ability to remember names, follow recipes, pronounce and find words, walk evenly, write, and see straight. I feel so pulled apart. The spaced-out painting in front of me represents the truth of what I feel inside. There are glitches, empty spaces in place of what should be connecting in my brain.

Hubert walks through the dining room, stops in his tracks, and asks incredulously, "Is that really how you feel?"

Softly, I utter, "Yes."

From the outside, I look quite normal, which is why moderate traumatic brain injury is often called the invisible disability. The missing pieces, my disabilities, are all beneath the surface.

As I sit quietly to consider my appearance in the painting, Hubert stands silently beside me and places a sympathetic hand on my shoulder. Perhaps by seeing this, he can better understand some of the gaps that are apparent in my thinking and our abruptly altered life together.

Looking at the spaced-out pieces of myself before me, I feel in my gut that this is the truth. I'm glad that Hubert can now see it, too. When the painting is dry, I bring it to

TBI Self Portrait: The Glass Fell, multimedia, 22×28. 1995

my counseling appointment. Hubert drives me to Fresno and brings a book to read.

The twenty-minute ride to Fresno to see Naomi, my therapist, always disorients me. The motion of the car seems to scatter my understanding, my speech, my wherewithal into thousands of fluttering confetti pieces. A quiet space and time to let the confetti settle is a necessity. Naomi and I sit and look at the painting in silence.

After a space of time, Naomi asks me, "Can you tell me about this painting?"

"Sure. I call it *TBI Self Portrait: The Glass Fell*. I prayed about what happens when glass falls and threw a mirror onto the ground to see."

"Um hmm," Naomi says, leaning forward in an effort to grasp each word. My speech is stilted.

I say as if telling a joke, "My friend, Gail, told me, 'Fado, don't you have enough bad luck without breaking mirrors?!'" We both chuckle. "I never thought of the bad luck part." *But it doesn't really matter to me because I don't believe it.*

"When I cut my picture into the same pieces as the broken mirror and spaced them out a bit, it felt true; it resonated within me. There are spaces ... " my words falter ... "blanks ... " my lips and tongue have stopped cooperating to annunciate and I spit out each word, "in" ... "my" ... "brain." There is much more that could be said, but it would be too much work in this present moment. I'm outta gas.

"I like the way your skin is drawn on paper and looks like a thin covering over who you are," says Naomi.

"Um hmm," I mumble. I have never before thought of skin as a mere coating to the me inside. Fact is, I'd been disappointed in the appearance of the cheap newsprint and how it stretched and bubbled when adhered with white glue. Naomi's insight seems to underscore the importance of expressing the real inside of me and not just keeping up with the on-the-surface stuff. *Getting beneath the surface is the uncovering part of recovering.*

After what seems to be a longer moment of silence, Naomi says, "It's interesting to me how the empty spaces of your injury appear to be like chains binding you."

Leaning my chin into steepled fingers, I study the image. I have experienced the empty spaces of my brain injury as vast nothingness and not knowing. To see these broken cracks within me as a source of being chained is new. "I hadn't thought of that before. But it feels true. Brain injury enslaves me."

I am body bound. At times I feel as though my body is a paper scrim covering the real me beneath. *What happened to me when the glass fell?* My body is bound by brokenness.

The tangible creative interaction of the Holy Spirit feels something like brushstrokes creating an image that will be disclosed at an unknown moment. Sometimes a brushstroke is bold and compelling, and at other times light and barely distinguishable. It is good to work with the Holy Spirit, whom the Bible also calls Counselor. In this painting the "brushes of the Spirit" reflects back to me, like a counselor, making visible the impact of an invisible injury. The Spirit is the One who reflects back to me my testing out expressions of what is real, the One who is able to fill-in the unknown blank spaces of my brain injury. I hear a promise in *TBI Self Portrait: The Glass Fell*. God assures me:

> *I will support you in this important work of uncovering what is real beneath the surface. My Holy Spirit will be your counselor in this important work of uncovering and recovering, your pathway to healing.*

8: Healing Headache
January 1995

I'VE MADE IT THROUGH ONE FULL YEAR of living with brain injury, and I want to know—no, *I need to know*— what this constant headache is about. It's something I've never lived with before and I hate it. I've suffered headaches before, when I've had a fever or flu. With my words stuck in the mud and mire of a headache, I decide to paint a picture of my headache, and give it to the Lord in prayer.

How do I paint a picture of my headache? When that glass fell on me, it seems that the impact caused pain to imbed deeply within my brain, in unknown ways. Perhaps the pieces of pain are lodged in the synapses, the message connectors of my brain, and have brought about a myriad of disabilities. *How can I paint this?* I have no idea.

By setting the alarm I keep to the one-hour up/one-hour down schedule prescribed by my rehab doc. But I can rarely make three hours a day out of bed, and my brain can only focus for around thirty minutes or so a day. I used to balance my checkbook to the penny, but now I'm five thousand dollars off. Hubert installs Quicken on the computer so that I can make multiple corrections and balance our checking account.

Fado, it's only a year after your injury. Keep to the rehab schedule, this will get better.

I don't spend much of my down time "discerning" what the Spirit's leading me to do with my painting of my headache. I simply pray, *Lord, lead me to complete this painting. Lead me to the truth. Amen.* The word, amen, is a Hebrew word in the Bible that has been uttered by both ancient Jews and Christians; it means "so be it." My amen—*so be it!*—has the weighty clank of a bank vault door, sealing away any wondering or focusing or discerning or belaboring. At surface, I want to believe that my spiritual-practice approach to painting my prayers grows out of my knowledge and education as a pastor. But at center, the reason I fell into prayer is because it is all I can manage. During my down hours with icepacks on the back, front, and side of my head, I do breath work, exhaling pain and inhaling comfort, working to move the stabbing out of my head, to slow the pain down, to deaden its fire. Sometimes it works; more often than not it doesn't. Stillness is akin to the frozen state of ice, and tempers the raging fire of pain. If I don't do it in spiritual practice, depression, the body's masterful way of icing down and slowing down, will do it for me.

So be it! I leave the mental process of discernment in the bank vault, and through my breath, work to reach stillness and a semblance of easing my pain.

Just before the alarm rings to signal my time to get out

of bed, an image of a headache wafts through me. I rush to paint this prayerful whisper before it dissipates. On a twenty-two by twenty-eight-inch masonite panel, I paint an underpainting with a mess of bright red, like blood from a blow, in the center. Waves of bright yellow, orange, and blue surround the red.

Through the few weeks of drying, I allow the question about my headache to steep during my moments of meditation. My headache has deep layers and brings to the forefront much that I don't know. There's a running joke in the family that when the glass fell on me I changed to become more like Hubert. I've moved from being left brained to right brained.

I had tucked away in an envelope the broken mirror pieces from my *TBI Self Portrait: The Glass Fell* painting. Laying out the pieces in an aluminum pie pan, I smash them into smaller shards with a hammer. The crushing blows send shivers through me because they echo my experience of the plate glass partition crashing into my head. *Yes, this is what caused my headache.* Wearing rubber gloves, I glue onto the painting pea-sized pieces of broken mirror splaying out from the central wound of red. Keeping the glass shards flat with glue on one side and the shiny reflective surface clean on the other side, is a painstaking chore, and it takes days. *Yes, this is my headache.*

On top of the dry underpainting with glued-down shards,

I create an overpainting with tones of yellow-green to blue-green, representing my consciousness, which comes to look something like the ocean. Using a palette knife, I scratch through the wet paint to reveal the bright colors beneath and create the weblike connectors of the synapses. In some places the synapses have circumvented the pieces of pain, making new connections. In other places the mirror shards block the connection entirely. The scraping and scratching feels like my headache. *Lord, teach me what this headache is about. I give it to you.*

Aisha is in kindergarten and Imani is a toddling two-year-old. I place the oil painting of my headache out of their reach, on top of the family room bookcase. It's not just the wet paint I'm concerned about. They could get cut by the painting. I hate it when my headache demands that I remove myself from the reach of my precious girls. So true ... *my headache doesn't bode well for curious little ones.*

Aisha and Imani sit on the floor of the family room and watch *Barney* on television. When we bought this house in Madera, the sellers wondered why we chose not to pull out the old carpet. With preschooler, baby, and dog I didn't want to worry about messing up a new carpet, and the sculpted, variegated brown hides just about every stain possible. Lying on the avocado green recliner with ice packs on the nape of my skull and my forehead, I pretend to watch *Barney* with my girls. I've seen this episode countless times. The girls think I'm watching along with them, but really my eyes are focused just to the right and above the TV, on my painting.

Gracious God, please teach me about this headache. Within my prolonged blank stare, the sunlight moves through the family room window, and the mirror shards catch the light. The entire painting changes, because the light illuminates the warmer yellow tones rather than the cooler blue tones of the green sea, and the mirror shards shine bright white rather than as a shadowed reflection.

Shivers cascade over my body. *Yes, Lord. The purpose of my headache is to cry out for healing, to catch the light.* In the Bible, the appearance of light is often a theophany, an amazing site of healing. Before this moment, I felt as though the purpose of my headache was to defeat me. This is so stressful to live with because I'm always in combat: fighting against my defeat. It is so much easier to live with a headache whose purpose is to cry out for healing. The "brushes of the Spirit" have shown me another way. The painting of an abysmal headache has been transformed into a painting about healing. I will call it *Healing Headache*.

Healing Headache, oil and mirror on panel, 22x28, 1995

Healing Headache

Sharp pain penetrating, emanating from a wound.
Synapses interrupted, detoured by the intruder.
Cerebral depths of the sea,
*   unchartered,*
*   powerful,*
*   life giving.*
Injurious cries for healing catch the light.
Undercurrents of ways unknown revealed.
Deepest pain reflecting brightest healing.

        —*Donna Fado Ivery, January 1995*

One of my classmates and study partners in seminary was a microbiologist Ph.D. Her retelling of the creation story from a scientific perspective inspired me. In Genesis 1:1-3, the Spirit of God moved across the formless void and face of the deep waters, and then God spoke the word and created light. Blue green algae, found on the face of the deep, are diverse microorganisms that have the genetic makeup to evolve into other forms, perhaps a basic building block of creation. The Spirit of God moved upon the face of the deep, and then, creation happened.

Spirit of God, move across the face of my deep,
the ocean depths of my brain, and create anew.
Heal me.

9. Beautiful Mess
February 1995

MY SENSE OF FAILURE is difficult for me to cope with, even more so than the chronic pain I endure. Deep down I remain an overachiever, perfectionist, and product of the Protestant Work Ethic. Good or bad, my discipleship is firmly intertwined with doing well to please God. I used to fear that my world would fall apart if I didn't do my best. Now I live in the free fall of failure.

I set the egg timer to one hour at a time so that I keep to my physiatrist's prescribed one-hour-up for every one-hour-down schedule. When I retreat to the bedroom, a growing amoeba of clean clothes remind me of my failures. Laundry had been my job. Now the bending over, standing, leaning, and forgetting is too much for me, and Hubert has taken it on. My part of laundry is washing, hanging out, folding, and putting away cloth diapers. From bed I have an unobstructed view of the corner chair with a mound of clean clothes spilling over. The igloo of laundry is large enough for an adult to hide beneath. *What a mess.*

The pile of laundry reminds me of my shortcomings as a mother. *So painful.* It is unavoidable, ever present in my bedroom sanctuary where I rest and renew.

9: Beautiful Mess

Yesterday I had a meltdown about the laundry. I behaved like a screaming, raging, contentious bitch. *Poor Hubert.* There are about four feet between the foot of our queen bed and the master bathroom. This means that I walk four feet without a cane and without surfaces to skim with my hand to keep balance. Each morning before school, helpful Aisha digs through the pile to find clothes for herself and Imani, and leaves scattered clothes on the floor. I can't bend over to pick them up. On the path from bed to bathroom, I can't balance myself and step around an obstacle course. When I almost fell I blew a fuse.

This just isn't right. I project onto him my feelings of inadequacy. He can't seem to do anything right, and I let him know it—way too frequently.

Hubert irons the girls' clothing every single morning. They are always clean and presentable for kindergarten and preschool. He works at the church and has taken on the many tasks of being primary caregiver for the children, and for me. And yet, my kindness and appreciation is running on empty. I have become less flexible—no, intractable. I'm drowning in chaos within and around me.

Earlier in our marriage, when Aisha was a baby, I learned to let go of many of my mom expectations like on-time feeding and matching clothing. In Hayward, Hubert once delivered, like a sack of potatoes slung on his hip, nine-month-old Aisha to me at the church office. Aisha was safe in the crook of his arm, parallel to the ground, lifting her curly little head to look forward, smiling because she was with her daddy. She had on a pretty red and blue calico dress with a Peter Pan collar, a white pinafore beneath the dress like a slip rather than an apron, mismatched socks and no shoes. I learned to laugh in such instances. The fact that I once locked the keys in the car, with Aisha strapped into the infant carseat inside helped me to pare back my childrearing expectations. Which is worse, mismatched socks and an apron worn as a slip or a child locked alone in a car? It was a lesson for me: I constantly worked hard to discern what really mattered rather than the way I thought it should be, and let the rest go.

Now my brain can't seem to do the work of discerning what really matters. I'm too much of a mess. Everything's a mess. I pray, *Jesus, help me through this mess.*

One of my rehab activities is to watch a television show and at commercial break have Hubert quiz me about what I'd just seen and heard—a simple short-term memory rehabilitation exercise. We no longer watch the news together because I shield myself from the world's heartache. I hold too much heartache inside of me to withstand more. On our VCR we taped a few painting and sewing shows on PBS. Not Hubert's topic of interest, but he barreled on through and watched a sewing show with me a few times. It didn't work out so well.

9: Beautiful Mess

After five minutes of watching "Sewing with Nancy," I press pause on the remote control and turn to Hubert. "Ask me something about what we've just seen."

"Well," he says with his gentlemanly smile and graceful gesture of his right hand, "Let me see ... "

Silence. *Doesn't he know that the longer the pause, the less I'll remember?*

Frustrated, I urge him, "Yes?"

"You know the things they put on the fabric ... "

"Pins? Patterns?"

"You know ... " he replies, fishing for the word he can't recall.

Raising my voice, I assail, "Don't you know that I don't know!"

Our TV-question rehab sessions usually ended in turmoil with neither of us better for the wear. Soon I adjusted the exercise to let him off the hook. It would be better that I do it by myself.

I taped a twenty-two-minute oil painting demonstration on how to paint a seascape. This PBS show is by a traditional oil painter who emphasizes technique. I like the colors: variations of sea-blue, pale yellow, white, gray, and melon-orange. I like the foamy surf, gentle tide, and translucent colors shining through the waves. The ocean tide reminds me that God moves things that I don't need to push myself.

I'm so tired of pushing and pulling. I hope that the "brushes of the Spirit" will imbed this painting with a serene seascape and this answer to my prayer: *Let God do the pushing and pulling.*

I press play and watch for five minutes. Pausing the tape, I do the steps as demonstrated. I squeeze out Titanium White, Ultramarine Blue, and Cadmium Yellow Light onto the paper palette. I know there are more. Which ones have I forgotten? I rewind, play, watch, and catch some of what I didn't remember. Pause. I squeeze out Ivory Black and Alizarin Crimson, too.

My painting lessons which are like short term memory rehab sessions, are replete with repetition.

- Play video for five minutes.
- Pause.
- Follow directions.
- Rewind.
- Play same video segment.
- Pause.
- Take note of what I forgot the last time.
- Follow directions.
- Rewind.
- Repeat.

Day after day, session after session, I pour myself into painting this simple seascape that a instructor completed in twenty-two minutes on television. He described this as a "beginner project," a painting that anyone can do. No matter how hard I try, what's on my canvas pad looks nothing like the teacher's. It looks ridiculous. Yet another failure.

My failures snowball. Failure of my short term memory. Failure of my relating gently with my husband. Failure of my soothing and nurturing my children. Failure of my managing laundry. Failure of my own serenity. Alone in the house, my frustration overflowing, I stand up at the painting table and yell out "Aaugh!" like Charlie Brown. With a palette knife I scrape up a glob of wasted paint from the palette and furiously spread it onto the failed painting. From the bottom up, I slather leftover paint onto the canvas paper, sweeping strokes in long leaflike shapes. Overlaying, streaking, dabbing color. As the intensity of my emotion is matched in the motion of my hand, I enter the Zen zone. A place of release.

Painting like mad, I'm done in six minutes. With cheeks wet from tears, I go to bed. I feel let down by the "brushes of the Spirit." God moving the surf in a seascape of serenity is not the answer to my prayer. Instead I have yet another failure to compound my chaos.

I've been asked to show two paintings at an art show at my parents' church, the St. Mark's United Methodist in Sacramento. Artwork must be framed for the show. I can't get a frame

Sleep, Pray, Heal

for less than thirty dollars for a twenty-two by thirty-inch painting on masonite. The cost is prohibitive. My sister Patty offers to shop thrift stores for inexpensive frames. She arrives from San Francisco for a visit today. The girls are excited that she is coming. Me, too.

After a time of greeting and excitement, we gather in the living room. Patty wants to see my paintings. Hubert brings them in, one-by-one, from the garage, bedroom, and family room. Patty brings in frames from the cars. Lots of frames, piled in the crook of each arm and in her hands. Aisha helps, and carries a frame, too.

I'm astonished by the number, and worry about the mounting cost. "How much do I owe you?" I ask.

"Three dollars," replies Patty.

"Each?"

"No."

My forehead scrunches, chin lowers, and eyebrows raise to ask the silent question: *Are you lowballing the cost to help me out?*

"Donna, I get the frames for twenty-five cents each, and there are twelve of them."

Whew. "Great. Now that's a price I can afford."

"Aisha, would you please get my wallet from my purse and give Aunt Patty three dollars?"

Aisha hops up gladly, gets my purse, and sits down on the carpet. She is pleased to do a big girl task like counting money.

9: Beautiful Mess

Patty sits in the rocking chair. I lie down on the chaise and position a pillow behind my head for support. Hubert props each painting against the desk, couch, and wall, and then sits on the couch. Patty is eager to hear the stories behind the paintings. But my hour-up is done, and I'm pushing it. My words harder to enunciate, I keep it short, pointing to each painting.

- "This is my pain. I call it *Pain*."
- "I call this *TBI Self Portrait: The Glass Fell*. I broke a mirror to see what happens when glass falls, and cut my picture into the same pieces."

Aisha gets up and moves close to Patty sitting in the rocking chair. She stands between Patty's knees and leans into her chest. Patty puts her arms around Aisha and pulls her in close. I continue.

- "This is my headache. Because the mirrors catch the light, I now see the purpose of my pain is to catch the light, to cry out for healing."
- "This is a landscape."

"It doesn't look like the others" Patty observes.
"I followed Bob Ross to learn how to paint it."
Patty nods. "What about this one?" she asks, pointing to the failed seascape.

"That's a mess-up." I say. I would have left that one in the garage. *It reminds me of a child having a tantrum scribbling in a coloring book.*

Patty exudes appreciation. "I love it. It's really beautiful."

For the next few days, especially during my lying-down-resting-time, my mind is fixated on Patty's appraisal. *What I see as a mess, she sees as beautiful.* I name the painting *Beautiful Mess.*

I can feel the "brushes of the Spirit" move within me when I ponder the beauty in the messes around me. When I focus on the beauty—in the perpetual mound of clean clothes, stack of dirty dishes, and array of stuff left around—I breathe more easily. It feels as if a window has opened within my homebound, closed-in metal box of failure.

The Spirit graces me with an *aha!* moment of insight: I couldn't paint the seascape because I was fooling myself. The answer to prayer I had sought was for Hubert to do more of the pushing and pulling, not God. I had been blaming Hubert for not doing the housework "right," or as I would. I've been blaming myself for failing, not pushing and pulling as I used to do so easily. God is the only one who can move the ebb and flow of the tide. I must get off of my habitual pushing-and-pulling bandwagon, ride the wave, and let God.

Beautiful Mess, oil on canvas paper, 18x24, 1995

So many of the paintings I have attempted are failures. In art therapy, when my intent is divorced from honest emotion, creativity suffers and the painting falls flat. In art and in heart, the creative Spirit only moves when truth abides.

I am assured that I could paint the seascape now because I am connected to the truth. If I were to prayerfully seek God as the mover of the tide and the waves, I could paint it.

Beautiful Mess

Words blend on a page.
Short term memory voids.
Physical balance and perspective of distance is uncertain.
My left side and energy drags.
One undefinable mess:
   blended,
      uncertain,
         dragging,
            voided.
Undependable leftovers: bearers of beauty.

                    —Donna Fado Ivery, February 1995

The next week my willingness to express gritty honesty during my meditation time is preempted by my drive to see beauty in everything. I am preoccupied with beauty, especially in the messiness of life. The song of my heart seems to be spinning on a record player, but I can't feel the groove because the record has been scratched. "Beauty, beauty, beauty," plays over and over and over and over. The nuance, flow, and feel of my prayerful duet with God stalls: It seems I am stuck and can sing no further.

My preoccupation with good denies Spirit's access to help me with the load of pain I bear. Not dealing spiritually with affliction increases my suffering. My days are heavy laden. My up hours eclipse.

During my prescribed down hours I try to see beauty—again, again, again—as if stuck in a groove on a turntable. My distress increases. I pray for rescue. *Lord, lead me to truth.*

Like the weight of the air shifting just before a rainstorm, the atmosphere changes. The spiritual presence of Jesus is palpable. My longtime friend and confidante, He is a welcome comfort. With a finely-tuned touch, Jesus lifts the arm of the needle out of the impassable scratch of my heart and gently places me in a different phrase of my song. In a wisp of a moment my honesty in prayer is restored.

We're rooting for the truth to win out in you. We couldn't possibly do otherwise. We don't just put up with our limitations; we celebrate them, and then go on to celebrate every strength, every triumph of the truth in you. We pray hard that it will all come together in your lives.

2 Corinthians 13:8-9 (MSG)

10: Rocking Lost
February-March 1995

OPENING THE FOLDING DOORS to the living room, I walk past the rocking chair to pick up something on my desk, leave quickly, and shut the folding doors behind me. I used to close the doors to keep young children away from mommy's work desk, but now I close them to avoid the rocking chair and all that it represents.

The accident cut off my ability to rock and nurse my baby. The rocking chair seems to hold onto precious moments of rocking and nursing Imani at any hour of the day and night. The rocking chair triggers my feelings of sorrow over cherished moments cut short, a monumental loss. I've taken to avoiding the living room and the rocking chair altogether.

My eyes and brain no longer track motion so that moving ceiling fans, tennis balls, cars, and rocking chairs make me nauseated and loopy to the point of falling over. Nodding my head up and down, shaking my head back and forth, scanning with my eyes to read, or walking—which involve surroundings moving across my eyes—all compound my headache. The pain in my head is constant, except for small windows of time when Vicodin abates my

headache just enough so that I can walk around without
bumping into the edges of doorways.

Lying down in bed, I settle my neck into the heavy
buckwheat pillow so that my head is completely still. I inhale
and exhale more deeply and slowly with each breath. Pursing
my lips as if to blow away the seeds of a dandelion, I blow
away thoughts cluttering my mind. *Breathe in love, breathe
out pain. Breathe in peace, breathe out worry. Breathe in
Holy Spirit, breathe out how to break up the steps to make
dinner during my up hour this morning.*

My goal is to reach the holy center of my being where the
extraneous activities of my mind are cleared away. Holy
literally means, "set apart." The tranquil space of my mind
is like a still lake, a mirror to the heavens. The "stillpoint"
is the Tao of the yin yang, the centerpoint from which all
creation and aliveness generates. The stillpoint is the black
hole, God's creative playground where re-creation, healing,
is possible. By quieting my body's chorus of dis-ease, I gravitate
toward emptiness and increase the space for my body's innate
knowledge of how to heal. At the stillpoint, my body's
mysterious ability to heal takes center stage. I seek the stillpoint
in order to reflect the mysterious and healing knowledge of
God. It's counterintuitive to invest in God's healing by
relinquishing my preoccupation with healing, but that's the

way it is: I must simply "be and let God." The stillpoint, the holy center, is the most powerful set apart space, where even quantum healing is possible.

But today I can't reach the stillpoint. I'm still pissed off by the rocking chair and all that it signifies: the inability to comfort and nurture my children, and possibly myself. So many times I have tried, as the African American Spiritual goes, to "Take it to the Lord and leave it there." I've been in a volley with Jesus, giving to him my anger and sorrow, and it bops back onto me, a monkey on my back. That rocking chair is wedged-in somewhere, barring the way of me reaching holy center. I argue with God.

You can take my job. Happened.

You can take away my pain-free days. Happened.

You can take away my ability to run, swim, ride, and drive. Happened.

Throwing down the gauntlet, I roar like a Mama Bear, *But you cannot take away my ability to nurture and mother my children!*

Arguing with God is a good thing. Arguing means I care enough about the other to deeply engage. Getting fed up and walking away is disengagement. Pretending to be at my best when inside I feel at my worst is disengagement. Speaking in socially courteous jargon so that I don't need to do the work of finding my own words is disengagement. Forgetting to call, touch base, and relate is disengagement. God is love, engaging cosmically and personally. I am convinced that God is pleased to hear me get mad and passionate enough to argue.

My entangling brawl with God leaves me with one thing on my mind. *I must paint a picture of that rocking chair. I will begin the long process of painting, expressing the honesty of my experience, giving it to God with each brushstroke.*

I didn't realize how hard it would be to take my first step. Going into the living room where the rocking chair sits, my heavy heart hesitates as I open the folding doors. The air inside feels weighty, even though the air is chilly from closing the heating vents to save money. Maybe it's because of the mucky emotional energy I associate with the rocking chair. The thick "ugh" of my heart hides in here.

Fado, you must express what you really feel about this. It's hard, but you can do it. You must do it.

I sit down upon the 1940s metal office chair with a ripped green pleather-cushioned seat and matching back support. The chair swivels and has a heavier and wider base than more modern chairs. Extra comfortable and sturdy, it's perfect for me, and I don't mind getting paint on it.

As I pause and sit still, the empty rocking chair plays its films of memories: Hubert and I shopping for a rocking chair, trying out a dozen varieties in a baby warehouse store. We were starry-eyed and excited about our impending parenthood. Because it fit us both and was on clearance, we decided upon an old fashioned pine chair with spindles, stained to look like cherrywood. More memories come to my mind: In the middle of the night Hubert singing spirituals to newborn Aisha, rocking her to sleep. Weaning toddler Aisha off the breast, cuddling her sucking on a warm bottle of water, the gentle sway of the rocking chair lulling her to sleep. Baby Imani in my arms in the rocking chair, drifting off to sleep, my nipple slipping from her mouth, the pouty center of her bottom lip rhythmically moving as she sucks her tongue in her sleep. Untold hours of my rocking and nursing my babies.

How do I express the truth of this?

Hell if I know.

I close my eyes and pray for God to guide me. My mind becomes like the dark green blackboards covered with white chalk that I loved to clean in the first grade. My words and next steps jumble, I wait for the blackboard to be cleared so that I can start anew.

After what feels like a long time my mind feels blank and empty.

On a twenty-two by twenty-eight-inch masonite panel I blend diagonal streaks of blues and grays. The colors alone are like the sterile plastic hook the obstetrician used to break my water when I was in labor with Aisha. The membrane protecting my feelings ruptures, and my tears pour forth, cooling the surface of my reddened cheeks. By just painting background blue hues, I am reminded of a shushed desire. In the ongoing drama of injury, I long for a backdrop of "the sky's the limit," fresh air, moving wind. *Lord, Jesus, I want to have a day that is breezy and hopeful.*

Drained, I swirl my brush in odorless turpentine, squeeze the bristles dry, and wipe the handle clean with a paper towel. I take a deep breath to strengthen my resolve. *I must do this.* I must express myself honestly. Excavating honest emotion takes whatever brain energy I have. I'm exhausted. I don't feel better. Rather I feel wiped out, a wrung-out washrag of tears.

A few days later, I brace myself to face the rocking chair hidden in the living room. This time I lay my hands on the rocking chair, adjust its position, and then sit and look at the assembled pieces of dried wood. What is my perspective? Again, I get up and slide the chair a tad to the right. *What is my perspective? How can I arrange how I see this chair and compose myself?*

First I need to see the rocking chair for what it is. Using the handle of my brush as a pencil, I try to sketch a temporary image into the wet paint background. But the blunt end is not sharp enough to cut through the layers of blue oil paint. I switch from the brush to a palette knife with a sharp corner and scrape-in a semblance of the rocking chair. I become persnickety with the positioning of my chin because what may seem to be a negligible change in my view changes my perspective. *Nothing is too small to make a difference.*

The palette knife scraping vibrates through my fingers, up my arms, and into my body that grates through me like fingernails on a chalk board. Startled, I shiver and manage to wipe the palette knife clean. If I were able to move quickly, I would run from the room, but I walk out, close the folding doors, and go to bed.

This time, an hour in bed is not enough to recuperate. I'm down for the rest of the day. Through the desert of muddled mind, I come to a ten-minute oasis of clarity. The scrape-sketch toll on my body is extreme, and the rocking-chair toll on my body is extreme. I've been running away from the rocking chair, keeping it behind closed doors, avoiding it all together. My perspective needs to change.

A few days later, I feel emboldened enough to again face that old rocking chair. In the now dry-to-touch paint, the barely discernible etching brings up my feelings of inadequacy. The sketch is wonky.

Warning bells go off within me and resound, discrediting my ability to proceed. *What makes you think you can do this? You are making a mountain out of a molehill. You know mothers whose babies have died. Compared to them, the loss of rocking your baby is nothing.*

At the Boston University Graduate School of Religion,

my most influential professor, Nobel Peace Prize Laureate Elie Wiesel, taught "Literature of Memory: Suffering and Faith in Literature," a life-changing course for me. Enrolling in the small seminar class required an interview with Professor Wiesel. My stomach lurched when I saw the Auschwitz prisoner number tattoo on his wrist. With meek and gentle mannerisms and a giant and compassionate intellect, Professor Elie Wiesel set the ground rules for the course: We are not to compare our sufferings. When we compare our sufferings, we naturally gravitate toward noticing one and not the other, belittling one for the other. I learned from Professor Wiesel that in Judaism, each of the great tragedies is numbered so that each stands with its own identity, voice, and merit, so that not one is lost or belittled through comparison. For example, with the Jewish tragedies of Sennacherib invading Judea, the temple destroyed, the diaspora, and the holocaust, to say one is the greatest leads to remembering the one. Human suffering is linked and one mustn't cancel out another. We discussed literary greats such as *Caligula and Three Other Plays* by Albert Camus, *Saint Joan* by George Bernard Shaw, *The Book of Lamentations*, in the Bible, *A Journal of the Plague Years* by Daniel Defoe, *The Story of Jepthah's Daughter* in the Bible, *Consolation for the Tribulations of Israel* by Samuel Usque, *The Possessed* by Dostoyevsky, and more. Every single utterance, each expression of suffering, every supplication of the human voice matters to God. Human tendency is to focus on one character suffering, but there are many more overlooked in the drama of literature and of life.

My mind is clear: *I must not compare my suffering to others'*. God desires to hear my own authentic expression, regardless of comparisons or artistic ability. It doesn't matter that I don't have the talent to complete a good painting. It doesn't matter that my suffering is not big enough compared to others'. What matters to God is that I authentically express what I'm struggling with in this uncharted course toward healing.

As my consciousness shifts, so does my ability to see where I have erred in representing the shape and contour of the rocking chair. With a blending brush I erase a few etched lines and redraw them with the palette knife.

Not perfect, but good enough.

The storehouses of my brain energy depleted, I go back to bed.

In yet another week, I gather the chutzpah to again broach painting the rocking chair. On the palette I mix mounds of light, medium, and dark brown oil paint, carrying the yellow, red, and brown hues I see in the cherrywood stain of the rocking chair. While speech and word finding feels like turning rusted gears, image and color flow freely. *Ahhh ...* painting is like diving into a placid, cool lake after hours of toiling in the hot sun.

I use a soft brush to replicate the smooth finish of the

rocking chair. The painting resembles what I see in front of me, but something is not right and I cannot put my finger on it. Now past my hour up, my energy and abilities have muddled, so I wash my brushes. Oil paints freeze well so that at anytime in the future I can use them without wasting expensive paint or remixing to match color. A painting palette is a staple in our freezer. To cover the palette, I pick up a box of wax paper to tear off a sheet, but my skewed spatial reasoning causes my finger to grate along the serrated edge.

It's a pretty deep gash. *Darn!* Drops of blood sprinkle onto the oil paint.

Oh well, at least the color of blood blends well with my color palette. The collage of cuts on my knuckles and fingers corroborate what I've noticed: my hands and fingers no longer go exactly where I intend, and it's much worse when I'm tired.

Damn! I can feel that I've been up too long. On the left side of my head, stabbing pain is increasing in intensity, getting louder and drowning out the other signals to the brain. I give up on my plan to get a glass of water and start toward my bedroom. Walking down the long hallway, I misinterpret where the walls are, my shoulder bumps hard against the wall, and knocks down framed family photos. The shocking sound of breaking glass catapults me back into the terror of the glass partition striking me and breaking the water glasses on the table. A blood-curdling scream escapes before I am aware that I have fallen onto the floor, my clenched body anchoring my screaming, shuddering, and shaking, my body tucked into a ball calling me to come back to earth and roll with it.

As if a lone voice calling from a rescue ship, I hear the words of Jesus, *Peace, be still* (Mark 4:39a). Grace, and only grace, evens my breathing.

I'm glad that nobody is at home right now. Mommy in this state scares my girls. *Hell, Mommy in this state scares me.* The earth-shattering, fatal-assault-screaming, out-of-my-mind floating is enough to shift the entire family system into dysfunction. I'm not as worried about me, because I know that Jesus will pull me out. I'm not as worried about Hubert, because he has strong emotional boundaries and won't allow me to pull him down. I'm worried about my girls and how much my brokenness will nurture brokenness in them.

My fall and post-traumatic stress wipes me out big time, and it takes me a few weeks to build back up to a one-hour-up, one-hour-down schedule. The rocking chair is unavoidable in my prayer time. Resentment encumbers my body, and I want to get rid of it. Beyond want, I *need* to release this burden. During my horizontal prayer work—what I call my down hours in bed—I visualize moving the weight of the resentment sequestered in my heart away and out of my body. It works like removing my finger in a glass of water. I can visualize moving the resentment out of my body, but the moment I move the attention of my mind to something else, I'm back to zero. Nothing works.

Expressing deep conflict is heavy work, no matter whether in painting, writing, or speaking. I sit in front of the painting and become familiar with it. I can tell it's my rocking chair, a good accomplishment. But something doesn't feel right. *What's true, Fado?*

Closing my eyes, breathing deeply, I pray, *Lord Jesus, lead me to truth so that I can heal.* My eyes glaze over as I stare at the painting, and I release my painterly concerns with every exhale. When I reach the stillpoint, the Creative Spirit nudges me and I am made aware that the smooth blending by a brush to capture the detail of the rocking chair doesn't meld with my unresolved and deepened sense of loss. What's true is that my loss is messy, uncomfortable, and uneven. With a palette knife I scrape in contours, layer on thick paint, and change the smoothly blended rocking chair into a roughly hewn one.

Yes. Here is my burden of loss compiled. Unbidden tears dust my cheeks.

Against a background of sky blues and purples with white sunlight streaming, a wonky image of my familiar rocking chair stands before me. Here is my burden of loss. But something doesn't feel right, and I can't put my finger on it. I'm spent. I give up. My inability to nurture and soothe my own children, as well as myself, is something that is too

heavy to move. *No matter what I try, I fail.*
The weight of my grief remains, deeply affixed.

My painting remains unresolved as my grief. I let it be and instead focus on surrounding support. Going through the motions, I seek out a frame for the unfinished-finished painting. I find one that is a few inches too large on all sides, and has a torn and filthy canvas painting wedged in and attached by roofing nails. The frame would fall apart if I take out the torn canvas. Rescuing the destined-for-the-garbage frame fits with what I want to do. I must rescue my mother-infant bond from being trashed by brain injury. Perfect for my rocking chair painting!

I have no idea how to make it work. Before my injury I would outline action steps to reach my goal. Such a task involves too much concentration, too much memory, too many steps, too much writing wherein words are mixed-up or missing. Now I take an alternative approach: during the wealth of my lying down hours I pray about it and ask the Lord to lead me.

The first step lands on my mind, not in the way of my figuring it out, more like a feather from above floating in. Of course, my first step is to clean the old frame and painting so that whatever I choose to do with it is possible. Glue and paint do not stick to dirt. With a scouring brush and diluted bleach I scrub down the filthy frame and ripped canvas. The splintering wood frame is too far gone to bear sanding. I wonder what to do next—but my mind is a blank slate. My brain energy tapped out, I go to bed.

After a few days of rest, I am in Walmart with my family. Shopping carts are great, offering me support, like a walker, but without the stares. No, that's wrong. I still get stares because I am a white woman with a brown toddler and five year old. In the San Joaquin Valley town of Madera, interracial marriage and biracial children are an oddity, a big *no, no,* to the culture of the town, which honors its rural identity, history, and way of life.

In the craft section I check out the clearance shelf. My eyes lock onto the cheapest pint jar there, a thick textural paint in the color of a warm pink with a hint of brown, trendy five years ago. *Aha! This is it!* For $1.25 I can use this paint to mask the splinters in the frame and paint over it.

I rest for a few days to recuperate from our trip to Walmart. And then I coat the frame with the textural rose-color paint. The sanded paint is too thick and will ruin my brushes, and so I use my hands and rub the paint onto the frame.

And rest for a few days.

Lord God Most Holy, lead me to complete this painting,

lead me to the truth. Amen. So be it! I don't have the wherewithal to figure out anything like this. I leave it there, in the bank vault for safe keeping, and move through my meditation for pain management so that I can procure up-hours with my daughters.

And rest for a few weeks.

Dressing Imani for bed in one of her footed blanket sleepers, she stretches out her little chubby legs and the material tightens against her shoulders. She's grown out of yet another one. *They grow up so fast.* I toss the too-small sleeper up onto the top shelf of the closet where a pile of outgrown blanket sleepers wait to be packed up and donated. *Aha!* I can use the fabric of the blanket sleepers to cover up the margin of the broken old canvas. I can sew a matte for the rocking chair painting, and it will be the perfect cost: free.

It's not that I haven't seen the pile of blanket sleepers at the top of the closet before. I have. I just haven't *noticed* them. So many answers to my prayers come in the form of raising something, someone for me to notice. My awareness is expanded. My consciousness is expanded. My *aha!* moment is Spirit's answer to my prayer, changing the scope and focus of my attention.

Could it be that those of my status and culture—white, middle class, American—have such a plethora of blessings and possibilities we don't need to call upon the Spirit's help?

But with my brain injury, I've had to rely upon the Spirit's help to merely get by. I know that I didn't "think of the blanket sleepers in the top of Imani's closet for the painting." I can no longer think of two things at once, and I was focused on changing the baby. When I pour the entirety of my brain energy into any task at hand, I cannot recall what I prayed for just a moment ago. Or, when I walk down the hall to get my checkbook in the bedroom, the task of walking erases the memory of my needing the checkbook. Or the task of pouring water into a measuring cup erases my count of the number of cups needed. To try to remember, I must sit down, be quiet, and ask for the memory to come, and perhaps it will lap toward me like a gentle incoming tide. One thing that brain injury has graced me with is a perception of when the *Holy Spirit* is acting on my behalf and when *I* am acting on my behalf. Noticing the blanket sleepers in this *aha!* moment is a gift of the Spirit, not my thinking. The painting wasn't in my mind's focus at that moment. It was another wisdom, another consciousness beyond my own that stepped in to help me out.

I acknowledge this new awareness, a gift of the Spirit, and rest. Sleep comes to me easily as I ride upon the gentle waves of the Holy Spirit.

Perhaps because the "brushes of the Spirit," is helping me with my maternal grief; perhaps because I am experiencing the Holy Spirit as a "Sweet, Sweet, Spirit" (a gospel hymn by Doris Mae Akers we sang at our wedding); perhaps because my sleep has been rocked by the gentle ebb and flow of the Spirit; I have an *aha!* moment. *The "brushes of the Spirit" feels feminine to me.*

I soon learn that my experience of the Holy Spirit as feminine has a strong biblical foundation. The Old Testament, often called the "Hebrew Bible," was originally written in Hebrew. The Hebrew word for Spirit, *ruach*, רוּחַ is a feminine noun, meaning "breath, wind, spirit." The New Testament was originally written in Greek. In Aramaic, the language Jesus spoke, the word for Spirit is feminine. In the purest form of the Holy Scriptures, the Holy Spirit is feminine.

The New Testament tells the story of Christianity expanding into the Greek world. Later, the work of Saint Jerome and Saint Augustine were instrumental in the gathering of diverse manuscripts, translating them to Latin, and deciding which ones were the accepted, inspired word of God. (393-419 CE). The earliest official bible, the "Latin Vulgate," was developed over a four-hundred-year span. In Latin, Spirit is masculine. The feminine Spirit of Jesus's speech and Hebrew Bible, and the ascribed fluid gender of Spirit in Greek, were circumscribed to be exclusively masculine in Latin, and then English. Language in Christian history has limited God.

The "brushes of the Spirit" moving within me has corrected the way I think of the Holy Spirit. From now on I will refer to Spirit as "She." God feels so much more whole to me when

I think of the Holy Spirit as She, Jesus as He, and the Creator as both Father and Mother: God is always so much more than any mind or language can fully grasp.

Wowed by my discovery that the "brushes of the Spirit" can correct centuries of church doctrine, I am even more eager to work with Her.

A heartbeat later, I get to work gluing the rocking chair painting, which is on a masonite panel, onto the torn, too-big canvas. Although I am looking forward to working with the blanket sleepers, the smell of the glue, like fingernail polish remover, is a red light. My brain has enough struggles and at all costs I resist any avoidable toxins that will damage brain cells. So I leave the smell and the painting behind closed doors and go to lie down.

I don't want to lie down. *Gee whiz, I lie down so much of my life these days. Is it a waste of time? No, it is a gift of time.* I try to convince myself that lying down and being quiet is an opportunity, not a punishment. I had planned to use my up-time today to play with the blanket sleepers and imagine how they can be manipulated to make a matte. *Damn it!* Everything takes so much longer than I expect.

Imani is almost two years old now and running around, and I'm still bowled over by the rocking chair and my sorrow over missed hours rocking her as a baby. *How long, O Lord. How long?* I do my breath work, inhaling light and exhaling frustration, inhaling connection and exhaling separation, inhaling calm and exhaling pain. My body and breathing and mind slow their pace, and I wait upon the Spirit, the Breath of God, to fill and transform every cell of my body.

A few days later, I scavenge enough up-hours to work on the painting again. *Joy!* Fun with art supplies! Sitting on the floor, I rummage through the pile of much-washed, pilled-flannel-footed blanket sleepers, and pull out those that are solid red, pastel pink, purple with dark pink arms, and dotted green and pink on white. Cutting out the zippers and feet so that I have as much flat fabric as possible, I lay the pieces atop the gross throw-away painting peeking out. The touch of the fabric brings back memories. *Damn this injury! So many precious moments stolen. So much lost.* I'm exhausted before finishing.

I go to bed, pray, and wait. *Lord Jesus, help me to uncover the truth so that I can recover. Teach me how to heal.*

Out of bed for an hour again, I walk out to our kitchen and family room for some recliner and family time. I glance at the rocking chair painting with draped blanket sleeper fabric on its edges. In the haphazard layout of the blanket sleepers I see cradling arms, and instantly my honest experience calls to me. *Fado, it's not the rocking chair you're mourning, it's your empty cradling arms.* I will cut and shape and appliqué the fabric into a matte of empty hands and arms. The worn out, pilled, grown-out-of blanket sleepers hold memory. Each sleeper is a different size, chronicling the stages of Imani's growth and the moments gone forever. This is about *Rocking Lost*. The uncovering of the totality of my prayer request is finally complete. The fact that I can see it now is God's answer to my seeking.

This time when I lie down, again, again, again, I feel a comfort that God is leading me through the unknown. A tune and song that we sang every Sunday at Marsh Chapel, Boston University, where I worked as a chaplain associate, washes over me. Who knew that a few simple verses from Psalms 4 and 5 would come to mean so much to me? This time when the words and tune transport me to a consciousness buoyed by assurance, I feel an ebbing sparkle of joy that these ancient words speak a cosmic truth.

> *Lead me Lord.*
> *Lead me in thy righteousness.*
> *Make thy way plain before my face.*
> *For it is thou, Lord,*
> *thou Lord only who makest me dwell in safety.*
> —*Samuel Sebastian Wesley, 1861*

On the living room wall, behind the rocking chair, Hubert nails a picture hanger and hangs the finished painting.

10: Rocking Lost

Rocking Lost, oil on board with quilted matte, 22 × 28, 1995

In a whisper akin to when I confessed my love to Hubert for the first time, I say, "I call it *Rocking Lost*."

"That's nice."

Argh! I wish he'd say something more, a bridge to sharing intimacy and the spiritual process I've gone through to pull it together.

Standing alongside him, I reach up and touch the blanket sleeper matte. "Imani grew out of these and can never wear them again. When I touch this I can remember all those moments," my voice cracks with emotion, "moments lost."

His arm drapes around my shoulders and his hand gives my upper arm a squeeze. His silent body language speaks volumes. He is here for me. I am blessed.

The most amazing, unexpected, incredible thing about painting the complicated layers of prayers in *Rocking Lost* is that the weight on my heart left my body and now resides in the painting. The monkey on my back has hopped off. So much of the unmovable heavy weight has been released.

The grief-bound energy of the rocking chair is gone, and now it's just a chair in the living room. The painting hangs as a memorial, holding dear the loss which I have not been able to throw away—*and should never throw away.* On days when grief overwhelms, I go up to the painting, touch the blanket sleepers forming empty cradling arms and remember. I have not given away or left my loss just anywhere. Rather, I have given it a place to reside in my home.

10: Rocking Lost

Another name in the Bible for the Holy Spirit is Helper. She has helped me to recover from *Rocking Lost* in a way beyond my imagination, in a way that is deeper than my thoughts or words. It is bizarre and mind-boggling that God communicates beyond words, and in a language accessible to me, which right now with brain injury, is art.

A similar thing happens when we pray.
We are weak and do not know how to pray,
so the Spirit steps in and articulates prayers for us
with groaning too profound for words.

Romans 8:26 (Voice)

Donna, Aisha, and Imani with *Rocking Lost*,
oil on board with quilted matte, 22 × 28, 1995

11: Possibly Never

April -September 1995

My position as senior pastor of the Madera United Methodist Church has been kept open for my return. In the meantime, two interim pastors have filled the job. The bishop needs to know whether I will be back at work July 1st, because the church needs a longterm pastor.

It is amazing that the church has been willing to go eighteen months with an interim pastor, in hopes that I will return.

I, too, still hope that I will return. My great-grandfather was a minister. My father was a minister. My cousin is a minister. God called me to be a minister when I was very young. My dreams, accomplishments, development, and identity are intricately integrated with "pastor." More than a job, pastoring is a vocation rooted within the flow of my days and thoughts as a disciple of Jesus Christ.

Preparing myself for a doctor's appointment during which I will raise the issue of my return to work, I tell myself. *Whatever the doctor says, you'll be fine. If you don't return to the Madera United Methodist Church this year, you can go to another church next year.* My tenure within the United

Methodist system graces me with assurance that when I'm physically able to return to full-time work, I will be appointed to pastor a church.

My physiatrist looks me in the eye, pauses, and says, "You do know don't you, that you may possibly never return to full-time work."

Stunned, I feel my heart seize up like a stone and sink. I am careful not to show any reaction. If I deal with the question of pastoring now, I'm sure my heart will crack open and shatter into a million bits.

Back at home, my seized-up heart feels too heavy to handle. I try to use denial to sidestep the idea of not being a pastor. But the words, "possibly never," distract me when I lie down, play with my girls, brush my teeth, and hang the cloth diapers out to dry. Possibly never—possibly never—possibly never: The words are a mantra within me that won't go away. To free my mind I *must* work through this. *Lord Jesus, what does 'possibly never' mean?*

In my prayer time I drift along a sea of consciousness as if I am in the survival float position I learned in Red Cross swimming lessons: stomach down with my arms and legs dangling in the waters. Lifting my head to inhale, "possibly never," enters my mind, and then as I lower and rest my head upon the open sea, I exhale and let it go. My thoughts release as I slowly exhale. Floating upon and facing fathomless depths beyond my knowing, I am drawn back into the Spirit-mover, the *a priori* source of my soul-self, the sparkle that created me.

> *In the beginning God created the heavens and the earth. The earth was without form and void, and darkness was upon the face of the deep; and the Spirit of God was moving over the face of the waters.*
>
> *Genesis 1:1-2 (RSV)*

The Spirit of God moving over the waters, creating something out of the depths, is the source of my renewal. This is the survival float for my soul. Suspended in prayer my insatiable need to figure out "possibly never" goes away. God knows and I don't, and that's okay.

> *For my thoughts are not your thoughts,*
> *neither are your ways my ways, says the Lord.*
> *For as the heavens are higher than the earth,*
> *so are my ways higher than your ways*
> *and my thoughts than your thoughts.*
>
> *Isaiah 55:8-9 (RSV)*

The moment I no longer need to know, images—gifts from the Spirit— float in and I rush to record them in paint.

Onto a twenty-two by twenty-eight-inch masonite board I paint a deep blue sky with Cadmium Yellow Deep and Alizarin Crimson tones for a sunset. Sunrise is filled with the possibilities of a new day. Sunset is filled with the never again of day's end. Sunrise and sunset are indistinguishable-mirror images of the other. "Possibly never" is indistinguishable, too.

Onto the sunrise/sunset I paint an array of puffy-white and threatening-gray clouds. Will my not being able to return to work this year be a season of tempestuous storm or clearing skies? Clouds are unpredictable. So is my prognosis. "Possibly never."

My head feels heavier and it's hard to keep it upright. My thought processes are weighed down, too—like tromping through a muddy swamp. I know that stabbing pain will follow, so I wipe my brushes clean, store my palette of oil paints in the freezer and go to bed.

My painted prayer about possibly never is incomplete. For the next week I prayerfully ponder "possibly never," yet I don't reach clarity. Not being able to figure something out bothers me. I *should* gain some direction so that I can get through this haze. The painting, my prayer, needs another level of something, but I have no idea what. I go back to my touchstone question that invites the Spirit's movement: *What is the truth?*

I don't know, and that's a problem for me. *Lord Jesus, how do I move forward when I don't know where I'm going?*
With the flowing energy of a lapping wave, I feel Christ answer my prayer: *Not knowing is the truth of possibly never.*
So this is my learning curve. My left-brain planning toward meeting my goal won't work right now. Laying out stepping stones of objectives so that I can reach my destination won't work in a swamp. I turn my focus further inward and drift on the sea of consciousness. No footing. No stepping stones. In my survival float, I face the depths of the unknown and my faith that the Spirit can make a way out of no way.
As I inhale, a scripture floats in:

> *Now faith is the substance of things hoped for, the evidence of things not seen.*
> *Hebrews 11:1 (NKJV)*

Jesus suffered the scourge of crucifixion, the finality of the grave, and the glory of resurrection. My faith in Jesus graces me with a perspective of hope through it all. The scripture reminds me to have the substance of hope even when I am unable to see any sign of hope on the horizon. I feel a calming light envelop me.
Suddenly I know what to add to my painted prayer about "possibly never." When I rise from bed I make a beeline to the sideboard and take out a single crystal champagne

flute, a gift on our wedding day. Hubert and I used this to toast to our love, hopes, and dreams. The uncertainty of my future as pastor is not the root issue of "possibly never." Beneath the surface I fear how my being too compromised to work will effect the health of my marriage, nurture of our daughters, and security of our home—our hopes and dreams for the future.

Onto the bottom-lefthand corner of the painting I add a gold-rimmed-champagne flute sitting atop a nondescript table. To paint glass, I barely paint it at all. With a liner brush, I basically outline the flute and add highlights. As I paint my mind drifts and I think: *This is the way prayer is—an outline form of an invisible reality. This is the way hopes and dreams are—with evidence as invisible as glass that holds substance. Without highlights, the shape of dreams and prayers are flattened.*

Inside the flute I paint a tightly-closed rosebud whose stem cannot reach the water. In church tradition, a rosebud is placed on the altar to give thanks for the birth of a baby. I wonder whether Hubert and I will be able to have another baby. We'd like to: But not with my limitations. Possibly never. Storm clouds brew overhead. Will there be a downpour that fills the glass and allows the bud to bloom? Will there be days of sunny skies and a withered rosebud? Will there be winds so swift that the fragile crystal flute smashes, our dreams destroyed?

11: Possibly Never

A few months later Hubert learns that he will be pastor of the St. Paul's United Methodist Church in South San Francisco. The parsonage there is less than half the size of our home in Madera so we downsize. Mom and Dad have come to help us pack for our move. They are pros at packing a kitchen and relating to little ones. We have also planned for them to transport my paintings so that they won't risk damage by the movers.

In the living room my paintings lean against the walls and furniture. Lying on the chaise, I watch Hubert, Dad, Mom, Aisha, and Imani pack my paintings. It's a collaborative effort. Imani and Aisha spread a bath towel on the surface of each painting.

I am so blessed by my family. Thank you, Lord.

Dad picks up my "Possibly Never" painting and says, "Donna, I haven't seen this one before. Can you tell me about it?"

"Sure," I reply. "It's about my doctor saying I will 'possibly never' return to full-time work. Sunrise is filled with the possibility of a new day and sunset is filled with the never again of a day that's done."

"What does the glass mean?" Mom asks.

"That's a piece of our wedding crystal. We used the champagne flute to toast to our hopes and dreams."

The room falls silent as all eyes are on the painting. In this moment, compassion is shown best by silent presence, and I appreciate my family's sensitivity. When the pregnant pause in the air is at is fullest, Dad asks, "I see a rainbow in the sky. Did you paint that intentionally?"

"No, I've never seen it before. *How on earth could I miss that?* He's right. The yellows and pinks of the sky are shaped in an arc. I would usually paint the colors of a sunrise/sunset with horizontal strokes. Most definitely, I did not intend to paint a rainbow. *The "brushes of the Spirit" added the rainbow.* I add, "I think the 'brushes of the Spirit,' added the rainbow to the sunrise/sunset."

The presence of the rainbow shines through me like a beacon of hope. In the Bible story of Noah and the ark, after the rains and floods ended, God made a promise to Noah.

"I establish my covenant with you, that never again shall all flesh be cut off by the waters of the flood, and never again shall there be a flood to destroy the earth." And God said, "This is the sign of the covenant that I make between me and you and every living creature that is with you, for all future generations: I have set my bow in the cloud, and it shall be a sign of the covenant between me and the earth."

Genesis 9:11-13 (ESV)

The bow and arrow was the weapon of Noah's time. The rainbow is the sign that God has laid his weapon down.

I relax within the auspicious message, God's answer to my prayer: Whether it is the sunrise or sunset of my ministry, hopes, and dreams, whether this season is brimming with possibility or overflowing with never, destruction is not part of God's design.

Possibly Never, oil and mirror on panel, 22x28, 1995

12: Coloring Family
October 1995

BRAIN INJURY EFFECTS THE WHOLE FAMILY. Painting offers a healthy way to express my turmoil and interpret the image in ways appropriate to Aisha and Imani's developmental stages. Imani understands that *Rocking Lost* is about my sadness when I couldn't rock her as a baby, and it hurts because I love her so much. Aisha understands that *Healing Headache* is about my head hurting and the way God helps me through it. Using art for expression opens the doors in my family for intergenerational understanding and empathy.

I am occasionally working through the *The Human Brain Coloring Book,* which contains medical-school-level diagrams and descriptions of the brain. I am teaching myself about brain anatomy and functions by color-coding the plates with a set of twenty-four bright markers reserved just for this book. Since my injury, I seem to be able to remember colors so much more easily than words, so learning the brain parts in this way works. Still, the book is way too complicated for me. I know that pre-injury I'd be able to read and understand it, but now I move super slowly through one page for weeks, one function at a time. Sitting in the green recliner, legs propped up, head and elbows supported, large paperback on my lap, markers and water to my right, I focus.

12: Coloring Family

The girls are always interested whenever I bring out *The Human Brain Coloring Book*. Coloring is in their wheelhouse. Six-year-old Aisha leans into the wing of the recliner, quietly stands and watches the open page and how I color.

Like a happy, positive teacher, Aisha pipes up, "You're doing a good job, Mommy."

"Thank you, honey," I reply in brief, trying to maintain my focus on the page.

She seems exceptionally interested, standing and studying quietly for an unusually long time. She asks, "What's the blue part?"

"It's called the occipital lobe. It's the part of the brain in the back of your head that helps you to see."

Aisha crooks her head, seriously considering what I have said, and then nods to let me know "That's good enough!" and skips off to play. She has a happy-go-lucky way about her.

Soon sweet two-year-old Imani mimics what her sister has done. A determined sparkle in her eye, feigning "I'm so old," she rests her cheek against my forearm and studies my progress.

"Mommy, what are you drawing?" she asks.

"It's a picture of the brain inside of your head," I answer.

Complimenting me in an exaggerated sing-song voice, Imani chimes, "That's good!" and with a mature purpose in her step trots off to find Aisha.

The girls decide to draw together at the dining table a mere twelve feet away. Big sister Aisha opens the door to my "office," a wardrobe right next to the table, and retrieves the mug filled with ballpoint pens and a wooden paper tray stacked with printed-on-one-side scratch paper. Ten minutes later, Imani leaves the table to play with her baby doll on the couch adjacent to my recliner. Aisha remains focused at the table.

I wonder what she's up to.

As if hearing my silent question, Aisha carries four sheets of paper toward me, announcing proudly, "Mommy, I made a book for you."

"You did? Would you read it to me?" I ask, closing *The Human Brain Coloring Book* and setting it on the coffee table at my right.

"Um hmm," Aisha says and crawls onto my lap. My arms naturally pull her in close.

The cover of her book, created on scratch paper, has a brain-shaped oval drawn in ink and crayons. *Wow. She sure was studying me. Who knew that a six year old would glean an understanding of the brain by watching her Mama color. Aisha's drawing is obviously a human brain!* Her studiously neat lettering spells out, "baningre by Aisha"

Aisha reads her book to me, "*Brain Injury*, by Aisha."

"I really like how you've drawn the brain, Aisha," I say, "I like how you've colored in the four sections."

"Um hmm." She accepts my compliment and turns the page.

Drawn with a ballpoint black ink pen, the second page has a big head with doughnut eyes, an open mouth with jack-o-lantern square teeth and lettering, "bran ing is not esey!"

She reads to me, "Brain injury is not easy!"

"Who is that?" I ask.

"This is you, Mommy!" Aisha retorts, completely aware that I have asked her the obvious.

"It sure looks like I'm having a hard time," I reply. "My eyes look a little crazy."

Her impish grin with a twinkle in her eye says clearly, "Mommy, you must know that you are a bit crazy with your brain injury."

She turns the page. This page has much the same face as the last, with the addition of a neck and, "blev me!" lettering across the top, and "go to your room" spelled out arched above the lips.

"Be ----leeeeve Meee!" Aisha reads emphatically. And then with a lower, louder, grumpier, and terser voice, she adds, "Go to your room!"

Troubling. A six year old's experience of a mother with head injury is "Go to your room!"

The last page has a rendition of the same face, this time with scribbled hair, football-shaped lips, and lettering across the top edge: "I do not now eneth adat hading but I now one then! Thay aer the most disks bugr in the." She has scribbled, "whut a pane" across the top of the lips.

Aisha reads, following her lettering with her finger, "I do not know enough about head injury, but I know one thing! They are the most disgusting boogers in the whole wide world." She adds in a whiny voice, "What a pain!"

"Thank you, Aisha. I love it!" I say, drawing her in closer and giving her a squeeze. "And I love you!"

There's a scripture about the church body, the Body of Christ, that I believe applies to the family.

> *If one part hurts, every other part is involved in the hurt, and in the healing.*
>
> *1 Corinthians 12:26b (MSG)*

Some may believe that children must be shielded from suffering, but I disagree. Children pick up on cues, and we don't give them credit for their innate wisdom. It's so important to honor them with the truth of the matter, within reason, in a way that they can digest. If I were to try to protect my girls from the truth of mommy's brain injury and chronic pain, this would be a disservice. The Holy Spirit works with truth, not pretending. My girls have the assistance of the *Spirit of truth* (John 14:17), to help them to deal with whatever is real. By shielding my girls from the truth I erect a barrier between them and the Spirit, the unparalleled wisdom of the breath of God with and in whom they innately share.

> *Jesus was matter-of-fact: "Embrace this God-life. Really embrace it, and nothing will be too much for you ... I urge you to pray for absolutely everything, ranging from small to large. Include everything as you embrace this God-life, and you'll get God's everything."*
>
> *Mark 11:22a, 23-24 (MSG)*

Brain Injury by Aisha Ivery, age 6

blev me!

go to yor room

I do hot no w ineth adaat hading but I now One then Thay aer The most dsks bugr in the

whut a pane

13: Hopes Dashed
November 1995

HUBERT IS IN AFRICA WITHOUT ME. We had dreamed of living in Africa as missionaries for at least three years while our girls are young. The United Methodist Church has a positive, long history in Africa, and has recently built Africa University in Zimbabwe. Hubert's dream is to teach there after completing his Ph.D. at the California Institute of Integral Studies in San Francisco. The area of his dissertation has to do with developing a *Spiritual Psychology* from the writings of the African American modern mystic Howard Thurman and an Afrocentric perspective. I looked forward to the experience of being in the racial minority and the opportunity for our girls to develop a stronger sense of their African heritage within their biracial identity.

Another hope dashed, for all of us. Damn this accident. How could a few scant seconds change my life so dramatically?

Eula flies in from Miami to stay for a week. Mahz flies in from Boston to stay for nine days. We thought that I could manage solo-parenting for the three days in between, especially with Aisha in the first grade and Imani in preschool. Last night was my first night solo-parenting since my head injury. Things went pretty well.

13: Hopes Dashed

"Mommy!" Imani runs through the front door and hurls herself face-first into my lap for a welcome-home hug.

Rubbing her back briskly, I say, "It's so good to see you! I missed you today."

Imani rests her left cheek on my left thigh, looks up to me, and beams. The dancing eyes and sparkling smile of a two-year-old melts my heart.

A few pats on my right thigh invite her to take a seat. Imani climbs up into my lap and sits up straight and poised. Perhaps she inherited her Victorian courtesy gene from her Southern gentleman father. For as much as Imani is a prissy little girl who loves everything princess and pink, Aisha is a tomboy who is suspicious of manners. In so many ways different, and yet the same, they both exude great joy and love.

Imani stretches out her little fingers to look at her bright pink fingernail polish. Yesterday, the first day of my being alone with the girls while Hubert is in South Africa, for a special activity I painted Imani's fingernails. Every so often, I notice her delightfully studying her pink fingernails. Demurely cupping one hand over the other in her lap, Imani is ready to talk.

"And how was preschool?" I ask. Each time she comes home from preschool, before she does anything else, she must get a Mommy hug and tell me one thing that happened that day.

"Good."

"Can you tell me one thing you did today?"

"I used the potty."

"Good for you! I'm so proud of you."

Her assignment done, she slides off my lap to go check on her baby doll.

"Hi, Donna!" my next door neighbor, Pat Drosky, calls as she climbs the stairs and comes inside. Pat is a member of Hubert's church as well as the chair of the personnel committee, hails from Oklahoma and usually sports a blond ponytail, cowboy boots, and a cowboy hat. She is driving Imani to and from preschool these three days, as well as checking in on me. *A Godsend.*

"Hi, Pat. Thank you so much for bringing Imani home."

"It's no problem! I'm glad to do it," she says, taking a seat on the couch to my right.

"I've got to tell you what's going on outside!" she says, chuckling. "Aisha just cracks me up! She and EJ are on their skateboards," the volume of Pat's voice increases with her exuberant storytelling. "EJ has tied a rope to the collar of his Dalmatian, and the dog is racing down the sidewalk, pulling him on the skateboard. Aisha's doing the same thing with Porter, and he's giving it his best, with Aisha going so slowly behind him. It's such a funny picture."

"That old man Porter," I say with a grin. Aisha and I have made up a song, "Old Man Porter," to the tune of "Old Man River." Porter is our first baby, a Labrador, Pekinese and Shih Tzu mix puppy we adopted from the SPCA. His conception, getting together a large and a toy dog, is a beguiling question. Porter is quirky in personality and looks like a grinning half-size black lab with a white tuxedo shirt. Since Aisha was born, Porter has been her playmate, protector, and shadow. The image of a graying nine-year-old Porter trying to keep up in the game makes me smile.

Pat relays the story with gusto again.

The front door flies open, and Aisha runs in and pulls a hemp rope. "Come on, Porter! You can do it!"

Porter slowly walks up the four steps to the front porch and then saunters into the living room.

"Good boy!" she says, stroking his back. Porter is panting and sweaty.

"Make sure Porter has fresh water, Aisha."

"Okay, Mom," Aisha calls. She's already in the kitchen, with the faucet running. And then just as quickly, she's making a beeline to the front door saying, "I want to go play with EJ some more."

"Okay. For one hour. We're having pizza for dinner tonight." Pizza delivery is a rarity, reserved for birthdays. Hubert being out of town rates for a special dinner and besides, being alone, I need to reserve my up-time for relating to the girls rather than fixing dinner.

Aisha's already out the door.

I call her back. "But first take the rope off Porter."

She runs back through the front door, into the kitchen, unties the rope, leaves the rope in the middle of the kitchen floor, and then flies back out through the living room to the outside. In her haste she has left the front door wide open, but Porter's too tired to leap at the opportunity for a freedom-from-people-and-leash tour around the neighborhood.

"So everything's going well for you?" Pat asks.

"Sure, thanks for asking," I say, but truthfully my headache is raging. I can barely keep my head upright with the support of the recliner, and I don't think I should talk to save my energy to manage the girls in the evening without Hubert. But I couldn't possibly tell the truth. Social convention requires so much pretending. It's exhausting. *Thank God that my prayer life requires honesty of heart and mind.*

Porter pads over and rests his head on my knee and looks up as if to say, *I'm exhausted but it was so fun. Tell me what a good doggy I am.*

With both hands, I scratch him behind the ears and firmly stroke his damp fur away from his eyes and down his neck, and say in a baby talk dialect, "Yes, you are; you are a good boy!"

Pat, sitting to my right, says, "Donna, is there something coming out of Porter's butt?"

Huh?

I pull Porter's hind quarters toward me and lift up his tail.

13: Hopes Dashed

Embarrassed, Porter tucks his tail between his legs.

Sure enough, there is a whitish gray two- or three-inch long weird stringlike substance hanging out his rear end.

From the kitchen I retrieve my yellow-rubber dishwashing gloves, and from the study area a trash can, and I sit down on a dining room chair without upholstery. "Come here, boy. Come here, Porter!" I call to him, in a way that guarantees a treat afterwards.

Porter stands in front of my knees.

Lifting his tail, and grabbing onto the stringy things with my gloved hands, I pull gently. The string seems to grow, and I pull some more, and more, and more. At least twenty inches of shriveled plastic masked with poop plops out and into the trash can. Aghast, it dawns upon me what it is.

Last night I changed a messy disposable diaper, the kind that gets taken directly outside to the garbage can so that it won't stink up the diaper pail or the house. After getting Imani bathed and dressed for bed, I looked for the diaper on top of the diaper pail, but it was gone. With my short term memory problems and the fact that it was evening, a time when info doesn't sync in my brain, I figured that I already walked the diaper out to the garbage but forgot that I did it. Or perhaps I had asked Aisha to walk it out to the garbage and forgot that I asked her to do it. This type of missing information, particularly in the evening, is standard fare.

"My Lord!" Pat exclaims, amazed at the length of this thing I've pulled out of the dog, "Do you know what it is?"

"It's Imani's diaper. I lost it last night," and then mimicking the old Alka Seltzer commercial I say, "I can't believe he ate the whole thing."

Next morning, I ask Aisha, "Where's Imani?"

"I don't know, Mommy" Aisha says as she looks up from changing her babydoll's clothes.

Getting up from the recliner, I take the short walk around the house. The parsonage is a compact three-bedroom, one-bath, nine-hundred-square-foot house. *I don't see her.*

Don't panic.

Where could she be?

Did she go outside?

No, surely you would have heard her.

I've been sitting in the living room where I can see both the front door and sliding glass door to the backyard.

I try to remain calm so that I won't frighten Aisha. "Aisha, maybe she's hiding. Will you go and look underneath the beds?"

With the demeanor of a surgeon ready to cut with a scalpel, Aisha searches.

I call out, "Imani!"

Aisha echoes, "Imani!"

13: Hopes Dashed

"Imani! Where are you?" My voice is becoming louder as panic sets in.

I search under the kitchen sink. In the laundry room. In the garage. Under Hubert's desk. Under the kitchen table. Under each bed. In every closest. In the doghouse out back. In the garden shed.

Outside, inside, we call to her, "Imani! Where are you?"

I call the police. "My daughter is missing."

"How old is she?'

"Two."

"How long has she been missing?

"Ten minutes."

"What is she wearing?"

"Red pants and a white turtleneck with little flowers."

"What is her race?"

"She is brown-skinned, biracial Black and White. She has lots of little braids."

"What is your name? What's your address? A patrol car is already on its way, Mrs. Ivery."

I'm thankful for all of the questions, as they serve to disassociate my mind from my body. *My stomach has dropped to the floor, but there's no floor.*

Aisha, crying quietly, sits on the couch.

We hear sirens, beacons of hope, and soon six patrol cars line up on our street.

One officer walks briskly up to the front porch to meet me.

He quickly confirms the information I had given to dispatch and asks, "Can we search your home?"

"Yes. Of course. Everywhere."

He motions for three officers to come into our house.

"Where is your husband?"

"He's in South Africa."

"When did he go there?"

"A little more than a week ago."

"Has she ever wandered off?"

"No."

"Would she go to the park by herself?"

"No."

"We're going to send a few patrol cars there anyway." Three patrol cars speed away to Orange Park, a block away from our home.

"I have a brain injury and sometimes I don't understand what's going on too well," I confess.

The officers' voices blare, "Imani!" as they search through the house and the backyard and then search again. Through the open sliding glass door I hear the patrol cars speeding through Orange Park just behind our backyard fence.

Numbness overtakes me and my legs have melted, so I sit in the living room, wait, and pray. *Lord Jesus, help us to find her. Protect her. Make her safe.*

And then I hear the voice of heaven in an officer's

13: Hopes Dashed

voice call out, "I found her!"

An icy splash awakens the numbness of my body and mind. Before I can stand up, into the living room the officer carries Imani curled up in his arms. She sleepily surveys the commotion and then realizes she is in a stranger's arms the split second before he hands her to me. She relaxes and cuddles into my arms. *Nothing has ever felt more right with the world than my little one safe in my arms in this moment.* Little beads of sweat create a headband along her hairline, and her clothes are damp with perspiration, and her skin feels hot. Her eyes now wide, she snuggles into me and rests her cheek against my breast.

"Where was she?"

"In your bed."

Damn! I don't think I'll ever make my bed again.

"It was really hard to see her. The bedspread didn't look disrupted at all. Do you want me to show you?"

"Yes, please," I say, and hand Imani to Aisha, sitting to my right on the couch. She needs the warmth and relief of Imani in her lap almost as much as I did. "Aisha, I want you to hold Imani for me."

Aisha is glad to be given the responsibility.

I follow the officer into the master bedroom. The bed is neatly made with a light-blue-duvet-covered down comforter, except for the triangle of sheet showing where the corner has been pulled back.

"She was asleep right here," he says, pointing to the middle of the bed, just below the pillows. "She was covered by the comforter."

I can just imagine prim little Imani sitting on the pillows, edging her little toes beneath the sheets, and sliding under the downy comforter without disturbing the elegance of a properly made bed.

"How could I have missed that?" I say, embarrassed by all of the work and resources expended because I couldn't see my own child asleep in my bed.

The officer offers me an explanation with a tone of consolation. "It was hard to see her. The comforter is so fluffy, and she is so small."

Yeah, right. Or it could be with my visual memory insufficiencies. I don't remember what I've just seen, and it's worse with stress.

Picking up on the officer's explanation mode, I say, "And she's a deep sleeper, but I'm still surprised she didn't hear us calling to her. We were yelling her name in this very room."

"We were, too," the officer said, "and then I saw a little movement in the bed."

After a stream of "thank you's" that cannot convey the depth of my gratitude, the officers depart as quickly as they came.

My mind, body, and heart now completely discombobulated by stress and exertion, I call my sister, Patty, to let her know what has happened.

13: Hopes Dashed

"I lost Imani ... and the police came ... and she was asleep in my bed." I say, struggling to enunciate and find the words.

Patty interjects, "I'm coming to pick you up. You're staying at my house tonight." Short and to the point, she hangs up the phone. Goodbyes are superfluous. We are in crisis recovery mode.

Aisha and Imani are delighted that we get to go to Aunt Patty's house in San Francisco for a sleepover. Patty puts me to bed, and I don't move. My well of energy drained dry by the crisis, I lie completely still, as if waiting for an IV drip of living water to restore me. *Jesus, Living Water, restore me, heal me.*

When I return home, I write a thank you note to the South San Francisco police. My Mama Bear antennae are on high alert. I vigilantly keep track of my daughters at every moment. But my efforts are futile as the icy-cold sheer terror of losing one of my little ones revisits me again and again even though the danger has passed.

Unresolved, in the pit of my stomach, lies a deep-seated shame because I am unable to care for my children on my own. I am stuck in the shame and the terror and the failure. I take it to the Lord in prayer. Not in words because they're too hard to find and remember and write down. Instead, I seek to share with God an image that expresses the truth of what I'm feeling right now.

Like a mason buttering a brick with cement, I use a palette knife to spread white, blue, and green paint onto a sixteen by twenty-inch canvas paper. My hand moves swiftly and the image forms in less than five minutes. This impressionistic painting is of a steep, icy, ski slope bordered by trees. The emotional pain of losing Imani, and the physical pain of my chronic headache make me feel as if I am stuck in peril, scaling the icy slope, tumbling down the snow-hardened mountainside, or falling at breakneck speed into the trees.

The Slope

A pain-filled day feels like
  either
painstakingly climbing up a
    steep
      sharp
        slippery
          glacier
  or
careening down
  out of control.
    There is no in between.

—*Donna Fado Ivery, March 1996*

13: Hopes Dashed

Pain-Filled Days, oil on canvas paper, 16x20. 1996

The "brushes of the Spirit" answer my prayer by playing through my mind a song I first learned as a youngster in Sunday school.

Rock-a my soul in the bosom of Abraham
Rock-a my soul in the bosom of Abraham
Rock-a-my soul in the bosom of Abraham
Oh! Rock-a my soul

So high can't get over it
So low can't get under it
So wide can't get 'round it
Oh! Rock-a my soul
                              —African American Spiritual

A pain-filled day is insurmountable, no matter my perspective: So high I can't get over it, so low I can't get under it, so wide I can't get 'round it. *Thank you, Lord, for rocking my soul through it.*

14: Broken Yet Whole
November 1995 - April 1996

WHEN HUBERT ARRIVES HOME from South Africa he has a lightness to his step and delight in his eyes. This was a trip of a lifetime. Lurking inside of me lies a profound sense of regret. Yet again, injury had caused me to miss out. *We were supposed to do this together.* I hide my regret beneath the surface, and above the surface I share my joy to have him home and that he has had such a great experience. My dad went with Hubert on this trip, and together they scouted out sites for an upcoming mission trip and tour of South Africa. They will lead a United Methodist tour there next year.

Hubert has brought gifts for us all. Necklaces for the girls. And quite a slew of gifts for me, an unusual amount, I think because I was on his mind while he was there. In both of our hearts, we grieved that I could not be in South Africa with him.

All the gifts he brought home for me broke.

- A small wooden table with a carved circular top and a foldable trio of carved legs. *Beautiful.* Two of its legs broke in transit.

- A hand-painted-ostrich-egg mug with a carved wooden handle and base. Broken into bits and pieces in the suitcase.
- An ostrich egg that feels like wholeness cast in porcelain. This was my favorite gift of all because holding it reminds me of the perfection of God's creation and brings praise to my consciousness. Nothing manmade could match the contour of its pristine shell. It broke when Aisha decided to stand on it. She felt so bad about it. Grandpa Don had shown her a picture of him standing on an ostrich egg at an ostrich ranch in South Africa, and he told her how strong they are, strong enough to hold an adult human or an over two-hundred-pound-mommy ostrich. *Amazing.* Aisha simply did as her Grandpa had done. A hollowed-out ostrich egg will crack when a first grader stands on it.
- A decorative-carved-wooden pot with a lid. Half the size of an ostrich egg, the decorative-dark-brown-wooden pot had carved figures on its rounded sides and lid. Hubert displayed it at church during a program about his trip to South Africa. Somebody dropped it, chipping and cracking both the pot and the lid.

So many broken gifts. I feel as though I am a magnet for brokenness. No matter how much I put on a positive demeanor —love my girls, love my husband, love my Lord, count my blessings—the weight of brokenness is heavy and presses me down. I am upset about the broken gifts from Africa, and this just isn't like me. *Material goods always pass away, so why get upset about them?* It's so much better to invest in people and experiences than in goods. Hubert's thoughtfulness remains unbroken in these gifts to me, and I am grateful. *So Fado, why are you upset about these things at all?*

Becoming overly upset is a sign that I need to take it to the Lord in prayer. In wipeout mode, I'm in bed for quite a few days. Perhaps because I was up more than I should have been while I was hanging out with Mahz and Eula these past weeks. The spoonful of sugar metaphor is true. For every spoonful I use in up-hours or energy expended, I need to lie down and wait for the energy to be replaced, spoonful by spoonful. There isn't any leeway. Up hours and energy are finite, *no doubt about it.* I'm up an extra hour today, so tomorrow I'll be down an extra hour. With Hubert gone, I was talking more, and that alone needs extra hours down to replenish the sugar bowl. At least while in bed extra hours I can attend to the Spirit moving, cleansing, and guiding me in my breathing out and breathing in.

Perhaps my hiding the weight of broken things has also slowed me down, a function of depression. *Lord Jesus, help me to unpack and resolve this weight on me from broken things.*

Blow out exhaustion, breathe in calm; exhale worry, inhale peace; breathe out stress, breathe in energy. *Holy Spirit, lead me.*

After a few days of what seems to be unending breath work, my mind and spirit reach a placid stillness, a pinhole of nothingness. Within the sacred space of unwavering quietude, I feel an answer to my prayer. *You are not upset about broken things; you are in turmoil over the broken gifts of your abilities.*

Aha … now this makes sense. The two-year anniversary of my head injury is next month. Seeking restitution for the damages we've sustained from the accident, we hired an attorney. He informed us that with brain injury, we should wait two years before filing a lawsuit because at two years we can see what disabilities, if any, are permanent. Brain injuries are slow healing, and it will be argued that many effects of such an injury will resolve themselves.

In these past two years, I've kept my outlook positive. Even though some medical doctors have proffered the "Nothing to do to heal this" line, by faith I've lived firmly rooted on the island of certitude that I will be completely and totally healed. But now with the impending two-year anniversary, I am overwhelmed by the knowledge that I have permanent disabilities from my head injury, broken gifts that are likely to stay broken. I've been so upset about the broken gifts from South Africa because they resonate with the deep grief I've been so good at sidestepping.

This is heavy stuff. No wonder I am feeling so walloped. Too big of a pill to swallow.

A fog of lamentation envelops me, although I keep up a positive face for Christmas traditions, school programs, cookie baking, ornament making, and family gatherings.

At the Christmas Eve evening worship service, in the darkened church, Hubert, as pastor, lights the Christ candle as the promises of the prophet Isaiah are read.

> *For unto us a Child is born,*
> *Unto us a Son is given;*
> *And the government will be upon His shoulder.*
> *And His name will be called*
> *Wonderful, Counselor, Mighty God,*
> *Everlasting Father, Prince of Peace.*
>
> *Isaiah 9:6-7 (NKJV)*

But for the first time I don't feel the glory within these words. A veil of coldness hovers over the promise of Jesus, and I can't feel the warming of my heart I usually feel in him. Instead, I feel numb.

When Hubert passes the light of Christ to the people sitting at the pews along the center aisle of the sanctuary, and in turn those people share the flame of their individual candles to those next to them, I feel nothing. As I hold the lighted candle in my hand and join the faithful to sing, "Silent Night, Holy Night," I feel nothing. Renewing my Christian faith, as is my ritual every Christmas Eve while holding the light of Christ, I pray, *Jesus, be born anew within me.* But this time my prayer feels perfunctory, a surface religiosity without rooting in my heart.

In the last two years of living with head injury, my Christian faith has been a Godsend. The "brushes of the Spirit" have answered my prayers beyond my imagination. Certainly, God has been leading me along a healing journey. I have truly believed that if my faith were strong enough, I'd be healed. I've clung to the words of Jesus.

"For truly, I say to you, if you have faith like a grain of mustard seed, you will say to this mountain, 'Move from here to there,' and it will move, and nothing will be impossible for you."

Matthew 17:20 (ESV)

Lord, am I not healed because my faith is not large enough? One hundred percent, I believe that the Spirit of Jesus can heal my disabilities. Certainly, it's me who has failed in the faith department. My beloved "Renewal of Faith" Christmas Eve Candlelight rituals feel hollow and empty. A pall of depression cloaks them. My faith has not healed me.

14:Broken Yet Whole

The month of January brings along even more horizontal hours in the day. Perhaps the wet blanket of heaviness is merely depression. It could be Seasonal Affective Disorder, commonly called SAD, the winter blues when the lack of sunlight changes the body's serotonin levels. A neurotransmitter that carries with it feelings of well being, low serotonin is a type of depression. I order some full spectrum light bulbs so that my body can better access light to fight the blues. My fair skin burns quickly, no, more than quickly—instantly— which equals not enough outdoor, natural sunlight time. Couple that with housebound days, and I'm a prime candidate for SAD.

Especially with the encroaching two-year anniversary of my head injury, and my attorney's understanding that my residual disabilities are permanent, Hubert and I decide to treat the date of my head injury anniversary as a special occasion. It's a difficult marker along my life's journey, and I know that my friends and family want to support me on a hard day. On January 26th we do something to celebrate life that we have not done before—we go horseback riding on the beach. About a dozen of us are led by a guide on horseback and for one hour we trot along the Pacific Ocean in Daly City, a mere twenty minutes from our house. The horseback riding place provides rider helmets and even a ramp to assist those with mobility impairments so I am able to get on and off the horse more easily. Although, my legs are dead weight when I get off the horse, so much that I have to sit down for awhile before I can stand supported by my cane.

It is a perfect day—family, fun, sun, and ocean followed by deli sandwiches at our house. Our head injury anniversary activity helps us to flip the "permanent disabilities," meaning of the date to a *Thank you, God, that I am alive and loved!* celebration.

Pretending that the two-year anniversary of my accident is just like any other day would not have worked. The "brushes of the Spirit" only move with truth, never with pretending. Facing a date with disastrous meaning, we asked for the Spirit of God to support us and knew that to do so we had to keep it real.

The "Breath of Life," as Christians have come to call the Holy Spirit, the most intimate essence I share with God my Creator, moves rhythmically within me. In my very breath God provides a process of casting off the old and creating anew.

Then the Lord God formed [that is, created the body of] man from the dust of the ground, and breathed into his nostrils the breath of life; and the man became a living being [an individual complete in body and spirit].
                                        Genesis 2:7 (AMP)

14:Broken Yet Whole

The "Breath of Life," the "brushes of the Spirit," work within a real human, within real life, not within denial or pretending to be what you're not.

A month after our horseback ride on the beach, no matter how hard I pray about my disabilities and the failure of my faith to heal me, nothing moves. It is as if the weight of a sack of potatoes won't get off of my shoulders. On Ash Wednesday, February 24th, I try to give the immovable weight to Jesus by painting it.

Ash Wednesday begins the season of Lent, the forty days before Easter when faithful Christians seek to move closer to the bold healing acts of Jesus that destined him to die upon the cross. The season of Lent involves sacrifice, denial, and extra study, and thus the tradition of partying hardy, as in Mardi Gras on Fat Tuesday, the eve of Ash Wednesday.

On the dining room table, I place a twenty-four by thirty-six museum-wrapped canvas, a canvas with modern, two-inch-deep paintable edges that doesn't need to be framed. I've learned my lesson—framing is expensive—and it's much cheaper to buy more expensive canvasses that don't need framing. Tucked on the bottom shelf of the dining room bookcase, I find a gallon-size Ziploc bag filled with the broken pieces of the ostrich egg and ostrich-egg mug. Sitting down on the dining room chair, I use my cane to drag the bag out and onto the floor. Bending over to pick it up, I lean my hand and shoulder on the cane. *Such an ordeal. Damn!*

Sleep, Pray, Heal

As I arrange the pieces of the broken gifts from Africa into the shape of a cross, I give the brokenness of my disabilities which have not healed as I have hoped to Jesus. This is my Ash Wednesday devotion: gluing eggshells onto a canvas, giving my broken gifts to my Lord. The term that my attorney uses, "permanent disabilities," is such a trigger word, looming in defeat, that I have not yet uttered it aloud. Instead, I decide to use "broken gifts" to describe those recently broken abilities that God graciously created in me.

When Hubert returns home from the evening Ash Wednesday service, I shuffle out of bed to meet him. I had asked him to bring home ashes so that I could make the sign of a cross on my forehead. Ash Wednesday ashes are created by ritually burning the dried palm leaves from last year's Palm Sunday worship. Instruments of our highest praise are burned into ashes of thorough confession. Not being able to go to an evening service, last year I burned some scrap paper to make the sign of the cross on my forehead, but it doesn't feel right.

The sign of the cross on my forehead on Ash Wednesday is like wiping clean my iPhone to its original factory settings, shedding all of the built-up software glitches. Out of the ashes I get down to my soul-self basics — I am created from the dust of the earth. In Latin, *humus* means earth, dust, ground. Humanity, humility, and humbleness are of *humus*, as is being down to earth. It is the breath of God moving through this body created of *humus* that is the origin of my life. I say the ritual prayer as I place the ashes in the sign of the cross on my forehead.

Remember you are dust, and to dust you shall return.
Imposition of Ashes Liturgy
From Hebrews 3:19B (NRSV)

The weight of the ashen cross on my forehead feels like a fly, and I want to swat it off like crumbs around my mouth after eating a crumbly cookie that I want to brush away. *This shouldn't feel normal, Fado.* With effort I resist touching the cross. Closing my eyes, I see on my forehead a burning shape of the cross that glows something like the fiery mark of Zorro. *God, this is so wild.* But it all fits with the intensive praying I've been doing today, giving my broken gifts to God. *God is at work in me, burning through the chaff.* The promise and light and love within this vision spills over into a stream of pure delight that flows through me, from the top of my head through my heart, and arms and fingers and torso and legs and feet. Basking in the power and love of God, I am happy, happier than I've been in a long time. *What a gift.*

"Let me help you," I offer to Hubert.

"Thanks," he replies, and sets down in front of me the pan he used for burning the palms.

In that moment I notice that he's used my good electric wok, a gift from our wedding. The heat of burning the ashes has turned the candy-apple-red-enamel coating to brown splotches and has warped the teflon pan beyond recognition and use.

All of the tears I've been holding back unleash. The dam breaks and I wail, "I can't believe you've destroyed it!"

"But I wrapped it in foil. I thought it would protect it," Hubert explains.

"Well, it didn't! Don't you know that you burn ashes in a disposable pie tin?!" I yell, fully aware that I am behaving like a condescending, raging bitch.

"I'm sorry," he says. "I just wanted a pan with a good lid for fire safety."

Between my tears I eke out, "It's just one more broken gift!"

Forty days later, my personal recognition of Good Friday draws me to put paint again on the canvas about my broken gifts. I could no longer attend traditional three-hour-long Good Friday worship services because I could not sit up that long. If it weren't for Good Friday, the day of the crucifixion of Jesus, I probably would have put off working on my painted prayer longer. *Who wants to unpack brokenness? Not me.* It's easier to sidestep around it. But the healing journey requires truth, and the Christian high holy days press me to go deeper, so I go to the garage to paint.

I stare at the stark white canvas on the easel. I am at a loss as to what to paint. *It's all just too much.* The light behind me shines onto the canvas and the arch of the dimensional ostrich eggshells form shadows on the canvas. Aware of the blood of Jesus on the cross this day centuries ago, I fill in the shadow spaces with bright red. Because Jesus hung on the cross for three hours before he died, I move the light, like the cast sunlight moved in three hours, and fill in the second set of shadows with a darker red. New wounds. Old wounds. *Lord Jesus, I give to you these, my broken gifts.*

I've overextended my up hours and feel my understanding careening down a hill of blur. Exhausted and ready to go inside for a long nap, I sit back in my chair, blow out, and look at the painted prayer in process.

Oh my God!

There is a new person, a new being, who is being born from the broken gifts. Not until this moment do I see that out of broken shells comes new life. *How could I have missed this before?* I remember as a preschooler visiting a chicken ranch, and as a second grader hatching baby chicks in the classroom. The "brushes of the Spirit" has blended with my painted prayer to create a new being that embodies brokenness. In front of me appear both crucifixion and resurrection, brokenness and new life.

Sleep, Pray, Heal

Lament of My Heart

Here I place my Broken Gifts.
    A gift of an ostrich egg from South Africa.
        Broken.
    A gift of a hand-painted ostrich egg mug from
    South Africa.
        Broken.
    A gift of ability to walk fast, hike, run, or bike.
        Broken.
    A gift of reading long without double vision.
        Broken.
    A gift of ability to ride, eyes open, in a moving car
    without becoming nauseated.
        Broken.
    A gift of ability to care for my young children
    and home without hired help.
        Broken.
    A gift of standing and walking with balance.
        Broken.
    A gift of a profession and years of schooling.
        Broken.
    A gift of stamina and energy.
        Broken.
Here I place my Broken Gifts.

14:Broken Yet Whole

The lament of my heart
echoes the rhythm of sorrow in the heart of God.
The Mother and Father, God,
who has given to the world a child,
a gift named Jesus
who died on a cross.
Broken.

Here I place my Broken Gifts.
On the cross.
Here my sorrow can stand.
Here my anguish shall not be relinquished
by those who cannot tolerate brokenness.
God can abide with brokenness.
With compassion,
God abides.
With open arms to share my suffering,
God abides.
With tenderness and a delicate touch,
God abides.
Here I give my Broken Gifts to God.
Now that I have given these my Broken Gifts.
Now that I have taken and placed these shells on a cross.
Now.
Now.

Now I can see
the shadows made by Broken Gifts.
Shadows filled with bright red of new wounds.
Changing shadows filled with dark red of old wounds.
Feeling shadows filled with wounds of precious gifts broken.

I grow to embody the shadows of Broken Gifts.
A new being, born from the broken shells.
    A body.
        A gift.
           On the cross.
Here, at the altar of my giving,
    I grow to embody.
Here, at the altar of God's giving,
    I grow to embody.
Here I am, a person growing into new life.
Here is the beginning of a new wholeness,
        that will not crush,
        that will not diminish,
        that will embody
           these my Broken Gifts.

           —Donna Fado Ivery, April 1996

I have painted my prayers, my questions to God about how
to understand/live with/deal with/deny/accept my permanent
disabilities and spiritual failures. The "brushes of the Spirit"

Broken Gifts, oil and ostrich eggshells on canvas,
24×36, 1996

moved strongly and answered.

In a heartbeat, through the movement of the Spirit, I have changed my definition of healing. No longer will I understand healing as "returning to normal." What is normal anyway? From observing U.S. popular culture and images in the media, we strive for a normal that is like a twenty-something-year old, lookin' and feelin' real good. This definition of healing leaves out so many of us. In the Bible stories of Jesus's healing miracles, the Greek word for healing also can be translated to English as "to make whole." Healing, wholeness, is available to me as a disabled person, a person who lives with chronic pain, a person who is not returning to normal. I have not missed the healing boat!

My wholeness embodies my disabilities and is a gift from God. In Christ I can claim it and name it. *If Jesus can rise without undoing the crucifixion, I can become whole without denying my disabilities.*

I am whole. I am healed. Thanks be to God!

15: Formed by Tears
March 1996

TWO YEARS AFTER INJURY, it feels so great to be able to preach again—and this time with some of my paintings. I so appreciate the message through image, perhaps because I feel such surprise and delight that God answers my painted prayers, perhaps because words exhaust me. My word finding and speech ability is profoundly better than two years ago, but the overabundance of words is a brain drain. I have limited fuel for all activities—moving my head, walking, speaking, and cooking—before my imbalance and stabbing pain in my head interrupts me, tells me to lie down. I remain on the one-hour-up/one-hour-down schedule as much as possible. But when I push beyond this limit, I pay for it.

I am paying for it now. I was up four straight hours to preach a few days ago. Sure, I arrived early. I lay down to rest in the pastor's office, then rose to speak and connect with the congregation. Hubert drove me home afterwards. The motion in the car compounded the brain drain of being up, moving about, and preaching, and I've had a jackhammer head and body like a wet blanket for the past few days. I need some handle of hope to get through this. Too blurry to think, I shuffle my way to the garage to try to pray with a paintbrush.

Sitting on a metal folding chair, I close my eyes, and breathe deeply to recover from my trek to the garage. To my right, propped up against the wall sits a thirty-inch-diameter circular mirror with hot pink and white striped edging, a Salvation Army purchase for Aisha's bedroom in Madera. Losing my job pressed us into losing our first home, and $38,000. We tried to keep it as a rental, but the costly property manager, damage to the property, and renters coming and going were too great of a burden. Hubert's new position as pastor in South San Francisco provides us a parsonage to live in that has less than half the square footage of our Madera home. Actually, I prefer this 900-square-foot house because I can hear the children at all times from bed, and I can make it to the garage and kitchen when walking is most difficult by holding onto door jambs and skimming my hand along furniture.

Opening my eyes, I look at the empty white canvas on the easel. *What feels true? I honestly don't know.* I wait for something, anything, to come. My mind is a fully saturated sponge, and I can't even absorb an idea. I look at myself in the mirror and burst into tears. *Too much pain for too long, dear Lord. Too, too long.*

I grab three tubes of oil paint and squeeze out blobs of a light-toned Alizarin Crimson, medium-toned Ultramarine

15: Formed by Tears

Blue and a dark-toned Prussian Blue. With a palette knife I sketch very quickly what I see: me in tears. Using my fingertip to paint the eyes, I finish the painting in five minutes. A title drops into my mind, like a stork dropping a baby down the chimney, *Formed by Tears*. Spent, I clean off my hands, go back to bed, and fall asleep.

South San Francisco is nestled on the Peninsula, between the ocean and the San Francisco Bay. Oil paintings will not dry in the damp and cool garage, so I hang them high in the warmth of the living room, away from inquisitive little fingers. The only possible wall space for drying paintings is directly across from the avocado-green recliner, the only chair in the whole of the house that supports my neck, arms, and shoulders just right. This means that I have to look at my paintings for the few months of drying time. *Ugh.*

The *Formed by Tears* painting confronts me daily, and looking at it, I feel like a failure. I have been practicing the discipline of "counting your blessings," like one of my favorite African American Spirituals attests. *Count your blessings, name them one by one. Count your blessings, see what the Lord has done.* I have been attuning my mind to the philosophy of *The Power of Positive Thinking*, a book by Norman Vincent Peale. I even bought the *Possibility Thinkers Bible* from a television evangelist. Being positive is a healing energy, and this is what I choose. I could have easily been killed in that restaurant accident. I am grateful to be alive! I count myself as blessed, for Hubert, Aisha, Imani, my family, my faith, my breathing, my food, my community, my haven of a home to live in. When a spouse changes dramatically due to brain injury, usually marriages don't last. Hubert has remained. I am blessed. *Fado, what are you crying for? Be strong for your family.* I *hate* the tears in this painting because they remind me that I am failing miserably at being positive.

After about a month of watching paint dry, the Spirit delicately reels me in to see something else within the *Formed by Tears* image. In this self portrait, a compassionate tension is evident between my strained facial features and the beckoning, moving, washing tears.

I feel the nuance of the Spirit's touch on my heart and feel Her intimate, patient question. *Donna, why are you ashamed of your tears?*

Huh? Am I ashamed of my tears? Yes. Because I interpret my tears as a sign of failure, I cannot see their beauty. In this painting the tears are beautiful. The lips and cheeks are stern from strain, but the tears, they bring a soft flowing nature to a stark image, my stark image of struggling with brain injury and too much pain.

My mind percolating, I invite one of my most trusted confidantes into my inner dialogue, the Bible. *What are tears anyway?* Salt and water.

In the Bible, water is always the threshold of new life. Moses and the Israelites pass through the waters of the Red Sea from slavery to wilderness. In the baptism of Jesus, he rises out of the water to a new experience of the Spirit, the delight of God, and self understanding.

When Jesus was baptized, he immediately came up out of the water. Heaven was opened to him, and he saw the Spirit of God coming down like a dove and resting on him. A voice from heaven said, "This is my Son whom I dearly love; I find happiness in him."

Matthew 3:16-17 (CEB)

A baby passes through the amniotic waters of a nurturing womb to her first breath and new life. Water is the threshold to new life. *Could my tears be a threshold to new life?*
Jesus preached,

You are the salt of the earth. But if salt loses its saltiness, how will it become salty again? It's good for nothing except to be thrown away and trampled under people's feet.

Matthew 5:13 (CEB)

Salt brings a zing, awakens my tastebuds, and enhances flavor. Salt clears weeds from pathways, ice from roads, and in my mind, cuts new trails for justice through the frontier wilderness. The mineral, sodium, is necessary for the human body to preserve a balance of water in our cells. Mahatma Gandhi led the Salt March to protest taxation and restriction of salt, necessary for survival in the heat of India. Jesus preached that we are to be salt for this earth.

Tears are salt and water, the stuff and promises of faith and life. Tears are holy waters at work. Through this painted prayer and the "brushes of the Spirit," I have changed my understanding of tears.

Formed by Tears

Welled-up eyes,
   so very deep in knowing.
Tears streaming,
   soften facial lines harshened by desert realities.
Tears flowing,
   wash my soul,
      awaken my connection to
   Holy Waters moving,
      above,
         below,
            about,

15: Formed by Tears

> *and within*
> *all living presents.*
>
> *Tears overflowing touch*
> *fullness of feeling,*
> *fullness of living,*
> *fullness of compassion,*
> *fullness of sorrow.*
> *Behold beauty by nature:*
> *I am a woman formed by tears.*
>
> —*Donna Fado Ivery, March 1996*

Many people have told me that they see Jesus in my painting, *Formed by Tears*. It took me a long while to see it, but now I do. I believe that Jesus was with me when I unleashed in streams of tears to wash my overwhelming anguish over chronic pain. Jesus, who endured the cross, is intimate with sorrow of sorrows and doesn't avoid my own suffering. When I hit rock bottom, Jesus is with me.

Sleep, Pray, Heal

Formed by Tears, oil on canvas, 18x24, 1996

16: Barely There
August 1996

"DONNA, I BELIEVE that all of your suffering will serve to make your faith stronger," a clergy colleague insists.

"Maybe ... " I answer meekly, covering up that inside I am taken aback.

At home and in bed I go through my spiritual exercises of releasing what I don't need and inhaling the expansive goodness of God, but I cannot reach stillness. I am consistently disrupted by the question of how my weakness may contribute to my spiritual strength.

In the New Testament, the Apostle Paul writes about his physical suffering, a "thorn in the flesh," that increases his spirituality, the power of Christ within.

> ... a thorn was given me in the flesh, a messenger of Satan to torment me, to keep me from being too elated. Three times I appealed to the Lord about this, that it would leave me, but he said to me, "My grace is sufficient for you, for power is made perfect in weakness." So, I will boast all the more gladly of my weaknesses, so that the power of Christ may dwell

in me. Therefore I am content with weaknesses,
insults, hardships, persecutions, and calamities for
the sake of Christ; for whenever I am weak, then I
am strong. 2 Corinthians 12: 7b-10 (NRSV)

Could my journey through physical wipeout, mental weakness, and chronic pain possibly make me stronger in Spirit? When I am physically weak, am I spiritually strong? Can I, like the Apostle Paul, be content in my weakness and rely upon God's all-sufficient grace?

The thought of suffering being spiritually good for me feels ... *so wrong*: masochistic, hateful, cruel, and evil are not characteristic of God, who is love.

In the past I have put the "suffering can be good for you" scriptures into an intellectual safe deposit box—shelved and preserved away from where I live. In the cultural context of much of the New Testament, Hellenistic Greco-Roman dualism separates the world into polar opposites: mind and body; Satan and God; heaven and earth; good and evil; flesh and spirit (In Greek philosophy spirit can mean psyche, mind, soul). Like the polarities of a magnet, counterparts resist or attract. If the body energy is suppressed, the energy goes to Spirit, and vice versa. Plato (427-347 BCE) separated the universe into dualistic counterparts. In the 17th century, so did René Descartes, the father of Western Philosophy. Dualism is a philosophical construct of the past, like a pair of eyeglasses, that can help or disorient. Knowing philosophical assumptions of ancient texts helps me to envision what they are saying.

The Apostle Paul, missionary to the Greco-Roman world, explains the Christian life in dualistic counterparts, or in ways that his Hellenistic audience can readily understand. In a classic scripture used too often in disability theology, Paul describes an increase in spirituality when our bodies—like earthenware jars—crack.

> *But we have this treasure in earthenware jars, in order that the extraordinary degree of the power may be from God and not from us. We are afflicted in every way, but not crushed; perplexed, but not despairing; persecuted, but not abandoned; struck down, but not destroyed; always carrying around the death of Jesus in our body, in order that the life of Jesus may also be revealed in our body.*
>
> *2 Corinthians 4:7-10 (LEB)*

Paul lays out polar opposites: afflicted/not crushed, perplexed/not despairing, persecuted/not abandoned, struck down/not destroyed, death of Jesus in our broken body/resurrected life of Jesus revealed in our body. When our bodies are broken pots, the imperishable spiritual treasure inside spills out.

I don't know. A colleague pressing me with good news

for my suffering feels detached from what's real in my daily, hourly, ever-present struggles.

Jesus, lead me to truth.

Unable to think anymore and my one-hour-down time complete, I walk to the garage to paint and pray whatever is honest.

A pitch-black background represents my state of not knowing and the pain-filled days when the familiar is obliterated beyond recognition. I paint a clear liquid medium onto the dry black surface and then add bright transparent oil colors: Alizarin Crimson, Indian Yellow, and Prussian Blue. I can't see the color on the black background or remember where I put them.

Lord, I just don't know.

I take a good look at myself in the mirror. I study the person reflected before me. *What's true for you?*

Using a palette knife I sketch with thinned white oil paint who I see in the mirror. Perhaps the white paint will pick up some blue color here, some yellow there, some red anywhere. Perhaps not. Unable to recall what color lies beneath, unable to plan or determine where colors will blend and move, I'm in a mess of *I don't know*. That's the truth, so I go with it and trust that the "brushes of the Spirit" will partner with me in my soul searching.

16: Barely There

I hope that this self portrait will look whispery-billowy spiritual, like popular-almost-transparent-glorious angel images. I hope that my suffering will make my faith stronger. I hope that a weakening of my body is energetically balanced by an increase of spirituality.

For a finishing touch I add a pop of orange hair, like the brown hair dye that has faded to an odd-brassy color on the top of my head. I should reapply a brown dye from the grocery store, but I haven't been to the grocery store for quite a while and asking Hubert to pick out a box of hair dye is asking too much. Lord knows what color he would come home with!

Emotionally drained and physically wrung out, I carefully walk the few steps from the garage into the house. Through the kitchen and living room to my bedroom, I skim the walls with my hand for balance and pour myself back into bed.

After an hour in bed, I return to the garage. Upon seeing the painting I stop dead in my tracks. The message in the image is loud and clear: *You don't look more spiritual. You look dead.*

For a few months the painting hangs to dry high on the living room wall away from inquisitive little fingers. Hanging directly opposite the only chair in the house that supports my neck, I cannot avoid seeing it. Slowly but surely truth distills, like the elementary school experiment of letting water evaporate in a small glass to find a sediment of solids left behind.

The "brushes of the Spirit" blow through me like a cool breeze on a blazing summer day. Does my suffering serve to make my faith stronger?

No. This is definitely not God's way of increasing my faith. Suffering and pain are bad. Period.

Suffering compresses me into being barely there.

Barely There

Body, Mind, Spirit, Soul: One Whole!
Pain thinning self:
  depleting body,
  weakening spirit,
  exhausting mind,
  stripping soul.
I become ghostly, eerie: Barely There.
I am still together here.
I am still together there.
Body, Mind, Spirit, Soul: One Whole!

—*Donna Fado Ivery, August 1996*

People rush in and want to help fix whatever ails me. Although my colleague intended to be helpful, her words, "Donna, I believe that all of your suffering will serve to make your faith stronger," were hurtful. Such words feel like a glib dismissal of my reality. Such words allow her to sidestep how I am really doing. Such words feel like a "pie in the sky" promise that distances her religion from me. This myth, that suffering and faith are energetically linked as polar opposites, is ensconced within the philosophical construct of dualism.

The "brushes of the Spirit" communicate to me through the image, *Barely There,* that there is another way. God does not dissect me into polar opposites. Spirituality does not distance me from what is real. God does not dismantle wholeness through it all. Nothing will separate me from the love of God, a promise and substance of superlative wholeness.

> *Who shall separate us from the love of Christ?*
> *Shall tribulation, or distress, or persecution, or famine,*
> *or nakedness, or peril, or sword?*
> *Yet in all these things we are more than conquerors*
> *through Him who loved us. For I am persuaded that*
> *neither death nor life, nor angels nor principalities*
> *nor powers, nor things present nor things to come,*
> *nor height nor depth, nor any other created thing,*
> *shall be able to separate us from the love of God*
> *which is in Christ Jesus our Lord.*
>
> *Romans 8:35, 37-39 (NKJV)*

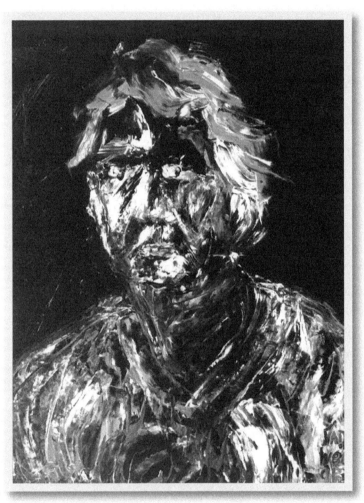

Barely There, oil on board, 18×24. 1996

17: Dormant
August 1996

LAST WEEK HUBERT AND I worked on cleaning out the garage. Overdoing has set me way back. For five days now I've been curled up in pain, waiting. Waiting, to spring back to my baseline.

This pain overpowers my senses and draws all my attention inward. The cries within my body have the effect of coating the outside world with a befuddling veneer. People sound like Charlie Brown adults, speaking with indistinguishable "Wah-wah-wahs." The pull of all my energy inward disrupts normal routines and family rhythms.

This morning I missed out on kissing Imani goodbye on her way to preschool because I just wasn't aware of the time of day. My exacerbated myofascial pain has added a dizziness and constant headache with an edge to it that is like chewing on aluminum foil.

It's four o'clock in the morning and I am wide awake. My frustration peaked to overflowing, I do the only thing I can when pain is too deep for words: I paint my prayer and allow the image alone to express my state. I look to spiritual depth and breadth beneath the surface to give me some handle of hope. It's true what Jesus said as reported in the Bible.

Look beneath the surface so you can judge correctly.
John 7:24 (NLT)

By sheer determination, I waddle to the garage, holding onto door jambs, kitchen counters, and chair backs for stability. Relieved to be sitting down in front of my easel—it's an easy reach to a garage-sale-find quasi-taboret stacked with art supplies—I find a primed twenty-two by twenty-eight masonite panel, set it on the easel and stare at the blank, white surface.

Dear Lord, what is true?

I paint what feels true: a naked, isolated and vulnerable me curled up in pain with a scrawny arm reaching upward for some sense of hope, for interaction, for intelligible expression. I paint me with all attention turned inward, confined to a pasty white body without sunlight, surrounded by dark red and navy blue.

That's enough. *Pretty ugly.* I need a break.

My painting oasis in the South San Francisco parsonage is a three-foot-square space in a tiny one-car garage piled with stuff: washer, dryer, and laundry. *Good thing.* It's a short walk to the kitchen door, and I can lean upon the washer and dryer on the way. Closing the door from the garage to the kitchen behind me, I pivot and perch my elbows on the microwave to catch my balance. I hold my head still in my hands. After the reeling in my head slows down, I open my eyes and see a few inches from my chin an aluminum pie pan with white rocks and rotting narcissus bulbs.

Instantly, I see a connection: These bulbs resemble the body I just painted. An astonishing *Aha!* moment. My pasty, curled-up, turned-inward body is like a bulb.

Finishing the painting, I add a pasty bulb close to my huddled body.

Now I understand the dark background as fertile ground rather than a lack of sunlight. The "brushes of the Spirit" planted a seed within me to make it through the harsh days. I can and will lie still in bed waiting, like a bulb in soil, waiting for healing, for regeneration, for new growth.

Pain Posture

Do not mistake my pain posture for a huddled hiding.
My body cries for me to turn inward.
My body-cries overpower outward signs,
  overturning external stimuli,
    creating soft soil in which growth occurs.

My body-bulb is an indwelling of remembrance,
  an invisible creation well,
    an active resource of wisdom and power.
Do not mistake my body-bulb for a huddled hiding.
Something good and whole is being born.

—Donna Fado Ivery, August 1996

17: Dormant

Pain Posture, oil on panel, 22×28, 1996

209

PART III: CREATING ANEW

Holy Spirit, truth divine,
dawn upon this soul of mine;
Voice of God and inward light,
wake my spirit, clear my sight.

Holy Spirit, peace divine,
still this restless heart of mine.
Speak to calm this tossing sea,
grant me your tranquility.

Holy Spirit, joy divine,
gladden now this heart of mine.
In the desert ways I sing—
spring, O Living Water, spring!

Andrew Reed and Samuel Longfellow, 1864
Holy Spirit, Truth Divine

18: Watershed
October 1996 - January 1997

My good friend from my church youth group and roommate in college is grieving the loss of her unborn baby. I want to be there for her in some way, but we live at opposite ends of the country. Words feel trivial and intrusive. In this moment, to speak of Christian assurance feels like dishing out platitudes. In the Bible, when Job was afflicted with insurmountable loss, his friends came to support him.

> *Then they sat on the ground with him for seven days and nights. No one said a word to Job, for they saw that his suffering was too great for words.*
> *Job 2:13 (NLT)*

Her visage floats in and out, like a lapping tide, in my devotions for days. I don't know of anything else I can do for her but pray. Other people want to be there for her, too, but rituals of support for a lost pregnancy, no matter how late term, are absent in our culture. Dear, sweet Gretchen must go to work and pretend that nothing has happened.

A week later, as I am decluttering the pile that has taken up residence at the end of our dining room table, I notice with new eyes the never-been-opened silk scarf painting sampler set. When ordering my painting supplies, I had needed to spend sixteen more dollars in order to save twenty-nine dollars shipping, and the sampler set was the right price. I've never been particularly interested in silk painting. I wanted to save money.

The "brushes of the Spirit" moves through me and I know instantly what to do for my friend. I will paint tears in motion on the scarf, in tones of blues and greens. Experimenting with silk paint on the two hemmed silk scarves, I'm in the Zen zone. The paint drips and blurs where the scarf is wet, and makes definite lines where the scarf is dry. Where the water pools, the paint colors dilute and blend into a solid, sometimes imperceptible color. I cannot predict how the paint will move on the scarf. I don't know what to do, with the paint, or for Gretchen. I trust that Holy Spirit will make a way and go with the flow.

As moisture wicks away and the silk dries, the paint continues to move. The piece appears differently than the wet silk scarf I finished yesterday. I had painted tears and now I see moving waters. The "brushes of the Spirit" speaks to me: *Tears are holy waters at work.*

Images come streaming through of what to write on the card that will go with this silk scarf. I am reminded of my painting *Formed by Tears,* and learning that tears are nothing to be ashamed of because they are beautiful. I am reminded of my painting *Rocking Lost,* and how helpful it is to have something, a memorial upon which to lay down the weight of grief. I am reminded how isolating pain is and how God is an ever-present help in the time of trouble. I am reminded how society expects pain to go away and grief to be done with too soon. I am reminded how spiritual resiliency builds when honesty collaborates with the Holy Spirit, who is a partner to truth. I am reminded how important it is to be a friend who can be a silent presence. All of these reminders culminate into a one page inspirational reflection. The scarf is created to offer comfort, care, and strength for her tears that are holy waters at work.

Thank you, Holy Spirit, for your flow and movement and way.

A few months later, I'm feeling insecure. I'm preaching this Sunday at my parents' church. Talking about my experience of brain injury feels awkward. It helps that projecting images of my painted prayers share in telling my story. Mom and Dad assure me that the congregation is eager to hear me preach; they've followed my progress, and prayed for me and supported them. Admitting my failures and inabilities is like airing dirty laundry and I feel dangerously vulnerable.

Hiding pain is normal. Presenting strength, no matter what, is normal. Sharing the experience of brain injury and chronic pain is not normal. And then there's the question of me preaching two services in one morning. I hope that my overdoing doesn't result in my staring blankly and waiting for a word to float in. The pulpit is sacrosanct, a bulwark of normalcy and privilege. I am no longer normal.

I am stressing out, winding myself up like a ball of yarn. Sensing the tightening within me, I pray. *Holy Spirit, lead me. Lord Jesus, I am your servant. Use me to do Thy will.* Like the playful swat of a kitten with a ball of yarn, I feel Jesus answer my prayer: *You've never been normal.* The divinely delivered thought causes me to chuckle. I let go and unwind.

A month ago I turned in my scripture readings and sermon title, "Healing Motions on Canvas: Brain Injury and Brushes of the Spirit." I remind myself that vulnerability in the pulpit is fine when it serves to preach faith. *Fado, this is not about airing dirty laundry. It is about giving testimony to the work of the Spirit.* I talk myself into relaxing.

My father calls me on Wednesday morning. "Hi, Donna. Is this a good time for you to talk?"

"Hi, Dad!" I reply. "It's a good time for me. What's up?"

"Fair warning," Dad says. "You're on speaker phone and we're in a staff meeting. We are planning worship for Sunday and the Strathdees want to know more about your sermon." Jim and Jean Strathdee are musicians on staff at the church where my father is senior pastor. I grew up singing their music, and have listened to their cassette tapes since I was a teenager. A few of their songs are known internationally, such as "I Am the Light of the World," and "What Does the Lord Require of You." Best of all, they are compassionate, caring people.

"Hi everyone! I'm looking forward to Sunday," I say, and give a quick synopsis of my sermon. "The John 14 Gospel Lesson is about Jesus telling the disciples that there are hard times coming, and he promises that God will send to them an advocate in the person of the Holy Spirit. Jesus says that the Spirit is the partner of truth who will reside in and remain with you. My paintings illustrate that truth and Spirit bring about a motion of healing."

Jim Strathdee asks, "Donna, can you tell us a little bit about the paintings you are going to share in your sermon?"

"Sure. All of the paintings are expressions of truth. They are a journal of my experience of brain injury. Whenever I touch a vein of truth, the "brushes of the Spirit" enters in. The Spirit brings about a motion toward healing. There's a painting I call *TBI Self Portrait: The Glass Fell,* which shares my seeking for the truth about what happens when glass falls. It's a portrait of me that I cut into the same shapes as the glass in a shattered compact mirror. Another painting is about when I searched for the truth about my chronic pain and I painted a picture of my headache. I glued mirror shards onto the painting to represent the deeply imbedded pieces of pain in my brain that interrupt the synapses and cause disabilities. When the painting was drying, the pieces of mirror caught the light and transformed the painting. The "brushes of the Spirit" showed me that the purpose of pain is not to defeat me. The purpose of my headache is to catch the light and cry out for healing. *Formed by Tears* shows how tears are holy waters at work. *Rocking Lost* tells the story of my not being able to rock my baby and has an appliqué of empty, cradling arms. It shares the way the "brushes of the Spirit" is a helper to bear the burden of grief. Another painting I call *Broken Gifts*. It is about my dealing with news that I have permanent disabilities. I glued the broken ostrich eggshells onto the canvas in the shape of a cross as I gave the broken gifts of my abilities to God. The painting shows a new person being born amidst the shadows of the broken shells. The 'brushes of the Spirit' taught me to change my definition of healing. No longer do I define healing as returning to normal. Rather, I define healing as 'wholeness.' I can now claim that I am healed, whole, and disabled." There are more paintings that I will talk about on Sunday, but I've relayed the gist of the sermon. Good enough for worship planning.

Pause. No one says anything. *Were we disconnected?*

I hear a voice resonating with sensitivity. "That's really powerful," Jim says. "Can you tell me a bit about the Book of Romans scripture lesson?"

"Romans 8:26-27," I paraphrase, "says that when we do not know—and with brain injury I have experienced not knowing—the Holy Spirit will speak for us. Or, in another translation, when pain is too deep for words, the Holy Spirit will take our prayers to God on our behalf. When we don't know, we have the assurance that the Holy Spirit will speak for us."

Pressed to end the staff meeting on time, as well as curtail their demands on my limited energy, Dad interjects. "Okay. Do we have any other questions for Donna?"

I imagine the staff shaking their heads "no."

Dad concludes the call. "Thanks, Donna. This has been helpful. I'll see you tomorrow."

The next day Hubert drives me one hour to rendezvous with Mom and Dad at the halfway point between South San Francisco and Sacramento. We have lunch and visit together at Wendy's. Then Mom and Dad take me and all of my stuff, including bulky original paintings, the rest of the way. When we arrive, I go directly to bed. My brain damage causes me to feel as though my body is still moving with the car even though now I lie motionless. I seem to not be able to distinguish the boundary between my body and motion. We've planned accordingly: I will remain in bed for the rest of the day and night. I do my breath work, exhaling the undulating churning waters that have claimed me, inhaling the tranquil peaceful waters Jesus brings.

> *Jesus stood up and commanded the wind and the waves to stop. He said, "Quiet! Be still!" Then the wind stopped, and the lake became calm.*
>
> *Mark 4:39 (ICD)*

By the next morning the gift of stillness has settled onto and into my body.

On Friday morning we travel the six blocks to the church (a short distance, so less proprioception fallout) and set up the slides and exhibit of paintings and poetry. Usually visiting preachers would set up on Sunday morning or late Saturday night. Such timing would cause a fallout of my already circumscribed abilities to speak, stand, understand, and walk. To procure intelligible up-hours I must finesse analogous down-hours. I've planned and communicated a schedule that will accommodate my disabilities:

- Friday. One hour set-up at the church in the morning. Practice and polish sermon. Rest.
- Saturday. Hubert and girls arrive. Enjoy. Rest.

- Sunday. To reserve energy I will not allow myself to practice my sermon in the morning. I will preach the first service followed by lying down and being still during the Sunday School hour followed by preaching the second service. Go to bed.
- Monday. We planned to have me preach at St. Mark's on the Martin Luther King, Jr. holiday weekend so that we can return home on Monday and Aisha won't miss school. I wouldn't be able to ride in the car for two hours after a big morning preaching.

None of this could happen without the unwavering support of Hubert, Dad, and Mom. None of this could happen if I were not bold enough to speak up about what I need. Hubert is taking vacation time to be with me this weekend. They all bend in ways to accommodate me. *Thank you God, for my family and all that they give.*

The worship building at St. Mark's United Methodist Church towers above the houses of a residential neighborhood in Sacramento. More important, the ministry of the congregation is a beacon to love and justice. A 1950s era sleek design with vaulted ceilings, pew seating for four hundred, the sanctuary is a space set apart for the sacred.

An hour before service, I arrive at the sanctuary. Scouting

out seats with neck support, I choose a pew along the outside aisle and lean my head against a cement column. Closing my eyes, I place my mind on "pause" and let go of any vestiges of things-to-do and things-to-think-about. Deepening further, I sense the quality of light, the smell of the air, and the feel of the room's volume. As I acclimate myself to the present, I set aside within me space for the holy. Now empty and fully present, I am prepared for the Spirit to fill and use me in worship.

Yet I am unprepared for the swelling to overflowing wash of the Holy Spirit that comes over me. Shivers pour out over every inch of my body. A warmth, something like direct sunlight, envelops me. Tears spring from my eyes. The choir of about thirty members, under the direction of Jim and Jean Strathdee, are running through their songs in the front of the sanctuary. With Jean playing the piano and Jim directing, the choir is singing a choral response that Jim has written to go with my sermon today.

Holy Spirit, speak for us,
When our words can't touch the pain.
Let your truth illumine all our lives,
And restore our hope again.

Spirit come and mend our hearts,
Heal the shattered mind and soul.

And receive our humble broken gifts
And make our spirits whole.

> *Jim Strathdee, 1997*
> *Holy Spirit, Speak for Us*

The lilt and movement of the music relates to my sensate being. The song's poetry tells of a prayerful relationship with the Holy Spirit. The voices and hearts of the choir create a harmony and energy of authentic worship. I am astounded by the intimacy of the words describing my painted prayers interweaving with Holy Scripture. My worries about the propriety of being vulnerable in the pulpit ebb away. I am stunned by overwhelming grace and beauty. I am ready to preach.

The worship services go better than expected. I don't remember the words I spoke. I remember the awesome feeling of surfing on the waves of Spirit. I've missed preaching. Today my soul has received a big welcome home hug.

After worship, the pastor stands at the backdoor and shakes hands with people as they leave the sanctuary. Since I am seated in a folding chair, my dad standing at my side, making eye contact while shaking hands forces me to lift my chin and bend my neck in a way that makes me dizzy. *I must get a barstool height chair to do this.* The blur of my mind and protest of my neck muscles cloak my senses. I'm not absorbing the teary-eyed responses of people as they shake my hand and express their thanks. I listen to them in a way that feels like overhearing someone's phone conversation: they express to me how much my sermon means to them, what kind of burdens they bear in secret, the "hopeless" feelings of friends, the relatives trapped by chronic pain, brain injury, and more. It seems that my willingness to share vulnerably gives others permission to do the same. Unabashedly clear to me is that there is a hunger for the ministry of Spirit to those in pain.

The next few days I sleep off my sprint of spent energy. In my increased down hours I work to empty myself and my mind and receive the spiritual resources only God can give. Although it feels good to be affirmed and to have preached strongly once again, I put it all aside like storing a good book on a shelf. I remind myself that no matter how well or how badly the sermon goes, people in line always say something good.

Dad and Mom call to tell me about the exciting responses they are hearing. The church office has received calls from a few people in chronic pain and brain injury support groups who heard about my sermon and want to buy a cassette recording of the service. Dad makes a laminated color page of my paintings to accompany each cassette. The office has produced more audio cassettes to fill demand. Mom and Dad produce a hundred videotapes of the service and sell them at cost. They sell out. The medical director of the

University of California at Davis Medical Hospital tells them my message is "portable."

Really, God? My experience of brain injury and chronic pain and the "brushes of the Spirit" is a message people desire to hear?

The next day, Gretchen calls me to ask me to make and sell the *Scarf of Tears* for others. As an oncology nurse, she witnesses dying and grieving. She has carried her *Scarf of Tears* tucked away in her lab-coat pocket at work and has found it very helpful. She believes it would offer help to others, too. It would be a way to be in ministry, working at home, a few hours here or there when I feel up to it. *This could work.*

It dawns on me that the sunset of my pastoral ministry as I painted in *Possibly Never,* is also the sunrise of a new ministry. I had not seen it before now. But the "brushes of the Spirit" did. It's in the painting.

Brain injury disability has been like a dam obstructing my vocation and who I am. I can no longer "go with the flow" of leading a local church anymore. The water of my training and vision for life has been stagnating. The whole thing stinks.

But today is a watershed moment. A small piece of the dam has broken through and a new flow and direction are mounting.

18: Watershed

Behold, I am doing a new thing;
now it springs forth, do you not perceive it?
I will make a way in the wilderness
and rivers in the desert.

Isaiah 43:19 (MSG)

Opportunities for ministry become revealed. The United Methodist Clergywomen's Association asks me to serve on a team to coordinate communication and edit their quarterly newsletter. Hubert and I start a home business, "Spirit Brush Art," where I work two to ten hours a month, dedicating myself to the Art of Healing. We develop a *Scarf of Tears* gift set to sell, each with a hand-painted silk scarf and self-published card. A few pastors who are comfortable with accommodations for my disabilities ask me to preach, and after the worship service I sell the *Scarf of Tears*. I preach at Wesley Seminary in Washington D.C. and lead a retreat on "The Art of Healing—A Spiritual Day Set Apart" in Maryland.

The pace of speaking, writing, and painting in my business is a gentle one. Each speaking invitation comes from a Christian with a servant heart who is intimately familiar with the needs of the disabled. I am surprised how accommodating people are willing to be. The hardest part for me is revealing and speaking up about what I need: rides because I don't drive, a place to stay the day before, a dark and quiet room with a pillow before preaching, somewhere to nap for two to three hours after preaching, and an extra day to recuperate from travel or a plane ride.

There is a river in the desert.

19: Dancing with Pain
January 24, 1997 - March 1997

WITH THE THIRD ANNIVERSARY of my head injury fast approaching, I feel the weight of the world slowing me down. My soul chants a dirge of a funeral lament, even though I try to counterbalance it with some blessing counting.

Gracious and Almighty God, I thank you for the gifts of:

- My husband, Hubert
- That I am alive
- Aisha
- Imani
- The brisk cold air
- The rhythm of my breath
- The sunrise
- That I have rehab'd my walking ability so that I can now walk Imani to kindergarten class five blocks away from home
- The fun of teaching Sunday School

The list fills up two pages in my prayer journal, but half of my days I still stay inside to recover from going out the day before.

Deep within, I feel that something more is happening, as if the rhythm of the moon and the stars and the tides and the days and the nights and the seasons have joined my funeral dirge. Traumatic anniversaries seem to join in a mighty chorus. January is damn hard. Recuperating from over-extended holiday up-hours is also in January. My body—beyond my mind—feels the looming anniversary of my brain injury.

Even three years after my brain injury, one-hour down for every hour up is an established routine, and I work on spiritual exercises at least a bit during every "do nothing" time. *Lead me, Holy Spirit.* I feel Her presence augment my deep breathing with an ionic richness. She restores the energy and purity of air like that of a rainstorm, surf, or forest. She cleans away the invisible and visible particles of smog in my breathing and being. Her palpable presence builds like a current, and I decide to flow with her leading. Like an archaeologist, I brush aside the dirt of the matter, and finally uncover a piece of deep truth: *Lord, can I celebrate life while being bound by pain?*

An image to paint rises to the surface of my consciousness: me, naked and vulnerable dancing with a body of pain. There isn't any protective barrier between me and pain; there isn't any protective clothing between me and the environment, so I must be nude.

My down-hour complete, I get up and make a beeline to the garage. For the benefit of the neighbors, it is good that our garage doesn't have windows. I undress and pose in front of the giant circular Salvation Army mirror that used to be in Aisha's room when we lived in Madera. In our much smaller South San Francisco home, there isn't any wall space for it in the bedroom. Hot-pink and white striped, the mirror has a 1970s vibe to it. Looking at myself in the quirky mirror, I sketch myself dancing with pain.

Hubert opens the kitchen door to the garage and is startled to see me naked.

With a flirty twinkle in his eye, he asks, "Whatz you doin'?"

"Praying with my paints."

"Why are you naked?"

"Because the Spirit told me to."

"Oh, okay then," he replies and shuts the door.

I love that man.

I quickly sketch on newsprint four nudes of me dancing with pain, but in all of them I appear to be falling over.

My will and determination deflate like a popped balloon. Rubbing my itchy nose wet with tears, I am overwhelmed by discouragement. *Your drawings show you. You can't dance with pain.* It takes so much work just to go to bed regularly and participate in festivities that demand more than I can give. *How can I enjoy life this way?* The burden of chronic pain keeps me from celebrating life, keeps me from dancing.

An hour wasted, I go back to bed and lie quietly. Each

Dancing with Pain, Sketch, pastel on paper, 18x24. 1996

score of breaths skims off a thin layer of compounded agony. After awhile my breathing feels less pressed by the weight of the ache, and I can add a mantra to each breath: *Lord, teach me how to dance with pain.*

A few days later I am in a bookstore with Hubert, Aisha, and Imani. I take a look in the Self Help section for books on chronic pain. One book, by a medical intuitive, looks interesting. I take the book in one hand and my cane in the other and walk around to find a chair.

No empty chair. *Damn it!* I am unable to read and stand at the same time. Maybe it's the movement of both my eyes scanning words and the ground always moving. Going through an anything-but-graceful process, I hold onto both a bookshelf and my cane for support and get down on all fours. Then laying my cane on the ground and gripping the bookshelf, I twist and plop my bum onto the floor with the force of sliding into home plate. Floor-sitting is a much better option than the toppling effects of standing too long. Pre-injury I would shop at thrift stores; now I shop at Nordstrom and other high-end stores for their seating availability.

Browsing through the book, I get its simplistic gist quickly: Our bodies hold onto pain because we have an emotional need for the pain to continue, because some part of our consciousness craves it. Instantaneously I am repulsed and my stomach clenches. *Could there really be part of me that wants this? Do I have chronic pain because I have an emotional need for it?* Closing my eyes, I settle in so that I can consider this hypothesis. Expanding my lungs, I inhale. I envision the life-giving flow of Spirit making a remarkable difference throughout my body on a cellular level. It's a mental picture similar to a high school biology class diagram with the red and blue veins representing blood cells filled or depleted of oxygen. Blowing out, I picture an animated wind, like on a Jack Frost cartoon, providing a gentle tide out of and away from me. Inhale: more cells depleted of oxygen are filled. Exhale: I envision the book, as if a surf board, riding on the low-tide waves of my breath, out and away from me. Inhale: *Fill me, Holy Spirit.* The Bible describes people of different nationalities and languages gathered in one, place and the Holy Spirit comes upon them like a rush of a mighty wind, fills them, and enables them to speak and understand one another.

> *When the day of Pentecost came, all the believers gathered in one place. Suddenly a sound came from heaven. It was like a strong wind blowing. It filled the whole house where they were sitting. They saw something that looked like fire in the shape of tongues. The flames separated and came to rest on each of them. All of them were filled with the Holy Spirit.*

19: Dancing with Pain

They began to speak in languages they had not known before. The Spirit gave them the ability to do this.

Acts 2:1-4 (NIRV)

I envision the Spirit rushing into me, like a waterfall, and believe that this will expand my understanding. Exhale: I place upon the gentle wave the judgmental stares of people who appear to be unable to abide with suffering. Inhale: God breathes life-giving breath into me. Exhale: I place upon the mighty wind the gelatinous moat of energy surrounding those who no longer understand me because of my chronic pain. There is such a vivid contrast between how many people relate to me pre- and post-injury, and it's painful. Exhale: blow it out. Inhale: expand. Exhale: release. Inhale, exhale. Expand, contract.

Finally, I reach Holy Center, a still lake that reflects God's voice. Relaxed, and centered, I am convinced of the answer to my question. *This is bullshit.*

I close the cover of the book and turn it upside-down on my lap because I don't want to advertise it. A wave of sadness flows from left to right in front of me. It is the sadness of those suffering chronic pain who must contend with such a book's ammunition. It is the sorrow of those in chronic pain who deal with the popular projection that chronic pain sufferers at some level choose to be in pain.

I've been sitting on the floor for at least an hour when

Hubert and the girls find me. Aisha and Imani join me on the floor to show me what book they have found to buy. With both hands, Hubert pulls me up to standing. An avid reader and lover of recently published books, Hubert has a few to buy as well. I prefer to use the library, especially for children's books, but since I cannot drive, I've had to let go of going to the public library. With all of the driving, working, and caregiving Hubert takes on, we've had to let so many things fall by the wayside. With my memory insufficiencies, library books have been lost and returned late, which erases the economical advantage. Oh well, there are worse things than regular family trips to the bookstore.

Little hand in giant hand, Hubert and three-year-old Imani stand in line to buy the books. Nearby, Aisha and I browse the Bargain Books section placed prominently for impulse buys. One book, *Anatomy for the Artist,* catches my eye. Leafing through it, I happen upon a page about how to add a sense of gravity to drawings of the human figure. Very simply, artists use gravity lines, vertical lines from ankles to neck to pelvis to hips to wrists. *Aha!* If I can add invisible plumb lines to my sketches I should be able to find the balance to dance with pain!

"Aisha, would you take this book to Daddy?"

"Sure, Mommy," she answers, happy to be asked. Her delight in helping runs deep, obvious when she was only a toddler.

"That's a big book!" she exclaims, surprised by its mass and weight. About twelve by twenty-four by two inches, the paperback is heavy.

"Yes, it is. It will help me to learn how to draw people."

Aisha is interested and pauses to study the sketched seated nude on the cover.

"Daddy and Imani are ready to pay. Hurry so that we don't need to stand in line again!" Aisha weaves through the line quickly, as only a child can.

Spotting an empty wall space framing the exit doors, I walk as rapidly as possible to claim it as mine, resting my back and head against it. To other folks I appear as somebody waiting. They have no idea what relief it offers to me.

A smile breaches my typically strained-by-pain face. The answer to prayer douses me with happiness. This is no coincidence that I've just happened to discover a possible answer for how to dance with pain, the question I've been praying about. This is the way Spirit works, with a nearly unintelligible butterfly-wing brush inside my solar plexus. I feel guided and delighted.

A few days later, I paint an abstract nude of myself in happy colors of rose, periwinkle, cream, mint-green, brick, and indigo. By inlaying gravity lines within my sketches, I have added a sense of balance to my body, just enough so that I

Dancing with Pain, 18x24, oil on canvas with mirror, 1997

can dance without falling over. There is an open space parallel to my figure for a body of pain.

How do I paint a body of pain? What is the truth? Who are you, pain? My questions are answered promptly, as if I have dropped in to office hours and asked my professor who is confident in the subject. I cannot adequately paint a figure of pain because chronic pain is not of my making. It is *other* than me. My body and my surroundings are of a created nature, and so I will be depicted in gestural brushstrokes. But pain doesn't feel created. Rather, pain is a foreign matter that is superimposed, placed where it is not meant to be. I will not paint pain. I will glue broken mirror pieces onto the painted canvas. Remembering the painted prayers of *TBI Self Portrait: The Glass Fell*, and *Healing Headache*, I will again use mirror shards to illustrate pain.

The finished oil painting hangs to dry in the living room on the only wall space available away from little fingers and unavoidably in front of my comfortable recliner.

Watching paint dry, the very definition of boring, avails the quiet space necessary for me to open to the Spirit's teaching.

Dancing With Pain

I do not choose to have Pain as my Partner:
  following my every step,
  bending my body to its intention,
  holding me always with cutting arms,
  tripping me up
    to fall fully into its blunt, harsh body,
  reflecting distorted and exaggerated aspects of me.
I do not choose to have Pain as my Partner.

For three years now, I've grown into knowing
  this Partner of Mine, called Pain.
I've caught onto just an ebb
  of a stunning, suspicious secret about Pain's Way.
Shh! Why the secret?
Perhaps the face of Pain is so gruesome
  my fear skedaddles over
  a cooperative character of Pain.

Pain follows rhythm.
  I step forward.
Pain steps back,
  for a moment,
    then lickety-split,
Pain steps forward again.
I overdo.

19: Dancing with Pain

Too many steps at once.
Pain cuts in.
I can "do"
*   as long as I keep rhythm with Pain.*
Pain follows rhythm!

With Pain As My Partner, I can Dance!
*   Sashay,*
*   triple step,*
*   step together,*
*   side-back,*
*   tap–tap–tap.*
*   Moving,*
*   rejoicing,*
*   feeling,*
*   the exhilaration of sheer freedom*
*   as body blends with breathless desire of soul.*
I can Dance!

It is a precarious, delicate dance I live
*   with this nasty Partner called Pain.*
But Pain knows and follows rhythm!
Therefore, I choose to improve my dancing skills.
I will outwit,
*   out-step,*
*   out-invent.*

I will keep up a joyous movement
  while keeping in rhythm with life's music,
  while keeping in rhythm with Pain.
Will I become so advanced that I will take the lead?

— *Donna Fado Ivery, March 1997*

In the first stanzas of this poem, I stand my ground and reject outright the assumptions so many hold about those of us who live with chronic pain. No, I don't want to live with pain. *No, there isn't any part of me that chooses to live in pain.*

In this poem I use Pain as a proper name, because this painted prayer teaches me that Pain is a someone, a body separate from who I am. I don't think I would have grown to understand the character of Pain had I not been painting my prayers. Each painting, more than twenty of them, depict the bottoming truth of my first three years of brain trauma: experiences uncovered, feelings excavated. Pain reflects exaggerated aspects of me, pushes me to blow my top, presses me into negativity, forces me into mind-numbing depression, steals my joy. In my daytime hour-down-for-every-hour-up lifestyle, I've learned about Pain's rhythm. My dance partner requires a turn to lead, and if I don't give Pain the reins regularly, like a paver, he'll roll right over and flatten me like asphalt. And yet, when I step back, refilling the empty well of energy, and allow Pain to take the lead, then and only then, will Pain let me step forward. With rhythm, dancing is possible; enjoying life is possible.

Dancing with Pain Close-Up

The spiritual process of healing is, at its base, uncovering truth. Jesus called the "spirit of truth" the Advocate.

And I will ask the Father, and he will give you another Advocate, who will never leave you. He is the Holy Spirit, who leads into all truth. The world cannot receive him, because it isn't looking for him and doesn't recognize him. But you know him, because he lives with you now and later will be in you.

John 14:16-17 (NLT)

Truly, the "brushes of the Spirit" is my Advocate, teaching me how to live with pain. In my painted prayers, I have learned that the Spirit moves only in those paintings in which I touch a vein of truth. I have needed to weed out my rush to make things appear to be normal, to cover up the reality of Pain's way. The spiritual work in my healing involves expressing honestly and looking for God's answers beneath the surface.

How do I discover the beyond-human-capacity balance required to dance with Pain? Like my sketch of me dancing with pain—leaning to the point of almost falling—I must use a vertical line as reference to discover balance. A weight on a string, a plumb line, is used to measure posture. A plumb line is used by builders to ensure that walls are vertical, because the force of gravity can cause leaning walls to collapse.

19: Dancing with Pain

In the Holy Scriptures, God shows the prophet Amos a plumb line in a vision.

> *And the Lord said to me, "Amos, what do you see?"*
> *And I said, "A plumb line."*
> *Then the Lord said:*
> *"Behold, I am setting a plumb line*
> *In the midst of My people Israel;*
> *I will not pass by them anymore."*
>
> *Amos 7:8 (NKJV)*

In the time of Amos, Israel was divided into a Northern nation and the Southern nation of Judah. In the North, King Jeroboam thought it politically unwise for his people to go to Jerusalem, see the glories of Solomon's temple, extol the virtues of King David, and dream of a time when the two kingdoms were united as one.

> *After seeking advice, the king made two golden calves and said to the people, "Going to Jerusalem is too much for you. Here, O Israel, are your gods, which brought you up out of the land of Egypt."*
>
> *1 Kings 12:28 (BSB)*

This is the context for the words of the prophet Amos to the Northern Kingdom. Amos speaks for God who is boiling mad, demanding righteousness, hating their religious rituals, promising judgment, and expecting social justice. The plumb line is a vision of clarity of right relationship with God. The convenient worship of idols led to the destruction of the Northern Kingdom.

Brain injury, for me, is to lean and be off-balance. Facing a lifetime of chronic pain feels like a forever trek to the tune of a dirge up a steep mountain. Leaning and being off balance, I can't do it. I need an invisible plumb line, one that only God can give, so that I can be upright for this path. When I feel myself losing balance, *immediately* I ask God to show me a plumb line. Stopping to look for God's plumb line, I am nudged to make adjustments. Sometimes I make the adjustments; sometimes I don't. Mindfulness at length takes a ton of focus. I know that God will add the energy, but still, it's so damn difficult to get off autopilot and create new habits.

The "brushes of the Spirit" is my Advocate, teaching me how to dance with Pain. God is my plumb line, giving me the balance to dance with Pain. Pain is the dance partner I don't want, the partner I must learn to dance with anyway.

In the first grade I had to hold hands with my dance partner, Jimmy. He was rude and overweight, with freckles and curly red hair. Although I protested, the teacher remained firm. I *must* hold Jimmy's hand for the folk dance performance.

At the Fado family dinners, each of us would share something about our day. I reported about how much I didn't want to dance with Jimmy. Both Mom and Dad took it as an opportunity to teach their four children how important it is to be kind to everyone, no matter their body shape or size.

"But Mom, I don't call Jimmy fat like the other kids. That's not why I don't want to dance with him!" Sue, Patty, David, Mom and Dad listened intently. "Right before we dance, he sticks his finger in his nose, shows me his booger, and then the teacher makes me hold his hand!"

Some dance partners are revolting, and Pain is a partner who is a sadistic arse. I'm stuck with him, probably for my entire life now, but I'm open to a switch!

20: The Storm of a Lawsuit
March 1997

I'VE NEVER BEEN INVOLVED IN A LAWSUIT before. I've never been in a systematic process wherein the sanctioned task at hand is to pick, pick, pick you apart. In 1996 we had filed a lawsuit against three parties who may be liable for the accident: the restaurant, County Building Inspection, and the construction company.

In both Reno and San Francisco I answered questions posed by the defense attorneys with my attorney by my side and a stenographer carefully recording each word. In addition to the expected questions, they asked me, "How is your relationship with the Lord?" and something like, "How do you reconcile 1 Timothy 2 and being a female pastor?" 1 Timothy 2:11-15 is the Bible passage most often wielded as a club to keep women down in the church. It says that women are to be submissive, silent, have no authority over men, and be saved through childbearing and holiness. The scripture is a letter from the Apostle Paul to his companion, Timothy. Together they took the word of Christ beyond Jerusalem into the Greek world and established churches. For the sake of the gospel, Timothy went to extreme measures, such as having his companion, Paul, circumcise him. They also changed their travel plans one morning because the Holy Spirit told them to do so (Acts 16:1-9). The love of God, the compassion of Jesus and the movement of the Holy Spirit have been calling women to ministry throughout the ages. Timothy changed his plans by the movement of the Spirit, and so has the church.

The defense searched to build the case that I have not healed well from the glass partition falling on my head because as the first woman minister in the conservative rural town of Madera, I took the accident as an opportunity to stay home with my young children. In the eyes of many fundamentalist Christians, such as the defense attorneys, and most likely the prospective jury, I had chosen the holier path as the submissive wife and mother.

The defense's medical evaluation found the cause of my troubles to be hysteria, yet again the ancient "crazy woman" diagnosis. My attorney told me not to worry about it. That's what the doctor had been paid for, to find some source for my problems other than traumatic brain injury.

The defense deposed a restaurant patron and witness to my accident who said I "flopped down" on the booth, which caused the plate-glass partition to fall. When my attorney questioned her, she was absolutely certain that I am Black. He pressed her further, asking her if there was a possibility that I was the only White person in an all Black party, and she insisted that no, I am Black. Her view of the accident was therefore discredited.

I am upset. This one-two-three punch case of the defense has floored me. My healing journey depends upon my being firmly rooted in the truth. I feel compelled to take a good look at each perspective about the how and why of my head injury, and to resist slamming the defensive door to others' insights.

- Did I really cause it by sitting too hard on the booth seat in the restaurant? I don't think I sat down any differently than I always do, and nobody has ever commented to me that I "plop."

- Could I really not be advancing fast enough in my healing because I love being home with my young children? Being with my girls is the only bright side to the brain injury upheaval of my life. But the shadow side is that I am home, but so often not with my girls due to the constraints of chronic pain.

- Is there something in my female DNA that responds more emotionally to a traumatic brain injury, and does this emotionality hamper healing? Two medical authorities have diagnosed me with hysteria. Could that be true? *Of course not, Fado. Why are you even considering the veracity of a misogynistic diagnosis?*

Considering such questions exhausts me. Instead of standing on a rock of truth, I am flailing around trying to find my footing in a deep sea. When talking on the phone to Mahz about how depressing these things are, she reels me back from the sea to an island of truth saying, "Fado. Listen to yourself. That is the most ridiculous thing I've ever heard!"

Taking part in a lawsuit demands meetings with our attorney. When a work commitment for Hubert conflicted with a previously scheduled deposition, I feel guilty because he is stretched too thin. Not wanting to do anything to prolong the already drawn-out lawsuit, we decide that I will go alone to this deposition in San Francisco. Hubert is wary, and I am, too. Every morning for a week, I write out and edit my plans for five hours in San Francisco on my own.

- Hubert will get the girls ready for preschool and first grade, thus giving me extra downtime in bed.
- Hubert will drive me to the attorney's office in San Francisco. I will arrive forty-five minutes before the appointment so that I can rest and regroup from the car ride.
- After the deposition, I will take a taxi to Patty's office in San Francisco. Or, I can first go out to lunch. It depends upon how I am feeling.
- At Patty's work, I will lie down on a mat on the floor and take a nap. She will bring me lunch if I haven't yet eaten.

- When I feel rested, Patty will take me to BART so that I can take the subway toward home, arriving sometime between three and five o'clock.
- I will use the payphone at BART to let Hubert know when to pick me up. On our way home we will get Imani from preschool. Aisha, playing at a friend's house across the street, will come home before dinner.
- I will bring with me an envelope with money to pay for taxi, BART, and lunch. Printed on the front of the envelope are the phone numbers for cab, Patty, and the street address for Patty's work office. Just in case I'm too looped to remember my home address and phone number, those, too, are on the back of the envelope.

In San Francisco, the deposition goes as smoothly and as stressfully as expected. With our meeting completed, in the swanky law offices on the top floor of a high-rise, I take in the head-in-the-clouds view. Shivers of adrenalin course through my body and congeal my focus and energy awareness; so I decide to rest and take advantage of the comfortable, high-end living-room-style lobby. Sitting on the supple leather sofa, I close my eyes and do some breath-work meditation. Too soon, I feel a startling impulse to leave, provoked by the "brushes of the Spirit" telling me that this isn't real. Opening my eyes, I see an extravagant view of the world situated above the populace below. *I must get back down to earth.*

After a long ride in the elevator to the bottom floor I again pause, this time in the shiny marble-walled lobby. Behind the reception desk sits a man in a uniform of a dark suit, shirt, and tie. *Should I ask him to call me a cab?*

No. You should walk in the fresh air outside first. You don't get to be free and alone very often. Take advantage of it. Don't let brain injury steal away this opportunity.

The law offices are toward the top of California Street, one of the steep hills for which San Francisco is renowned. As I walk downhill I pace and balance myself with my cane. The cool, brisk air feels refreshing on my face and in my lungs. Being in the mix of the hustle and bustle of city life feels like a vacation away from being a homebody—being a homebody is something that doesn't come naturally to me.

Two blocks down the hill I stop at a quaint restaurant with a patio and tables filled with customers. A packed restaurant is a sign of good food and quality, so I go inside. Going out to lunch is an event for me, another experience with a vacation-like thrill. But when I see the inflated prices, I leave.

You've got to stop and rest.

I will. Let me just find a good spot.

Walking another three blocks down the hill, I feel loopy. I stop to rest by a modern fountain with an amphitheater-like surround. People sit on bench-like-steps, eat sack lunches and visit. Some feed the pigeons. Sitting on the firm, cold seat, I rest and people-watch, but there isn't any support for my neck or back, so my need to rest is unfulfilled and tempering chronic pain hijacked. *Oh well. Keep on walking. You will find a place to eat and rest and call a cab.*

Although the blurriness of my mind tells me that it's time to call a cab, I don't want to end my respite of independence. *To be free! Ahh.* I walk further down the hill and come to a coffee bar with a booming to-go business. Standing in a long line, leaning on my cane, I struggle to keep myself upright because my body seems to be weaving. Finally getting to the counter, I order a coffee and toasted bagel with cream cheese, and ask if someone can call me a cab. The cashier looks at me as if my request is one of supreme inconvenience and would unfairly jeopardize every customer in line behind me. In an unapologetic and condescending tone she says, "Customers don't really have access to a phone here."

In as cheery a voice I can muster I say, "That's okay."

Because I need two hands to open the envelope with cash, I lean both my cane and front against the counter. She looks perturbed. So that I can walk with cane in one hand and cup of coffee in the other, I must take the time to put the bag with the toasted bagel with cream cheese into my purse before I grab the coffee waiting on the counter. Now she's glaring at me, completely fed up.

With my face reddening in humiliation, I leave as quickly as I can and look for a place with back and neck support to sit down and eat. Scanning the area, for something—anything—nearby, I see a broader sidewalk space by the building. Sitting down crosslegged and leaning my back and head against the building, I try to ignore the smell of pee, pretty common in urban areas, and wonder if I'm sitting on dried urine. *Just do this. You have to eat. You have to rest to regroup.* After only a few bites of bagel and sips of coffee, I rewrap the bagel and store it in my purse. The ammonia smell of urine is affecting the taste.

Taking care not to depend on my weakened left side, I brace myself on both the cane and wall to stand. I look at the coffee cup on the sidewalk. I know that if I bend down to pick it up, I will fall. I choose to leave it there. It feels so wrong to litter. Standing, leaning against the wall, I look to see if there's a passerby whom I can ask to pick up the cup and hand it to me. But everyone is watching the sidewalk, seeming to be in a rush. Ashamed, I leave my coffee cup on the sidewalk and set out down the hill.

You should lie down and rest, Fado.

It's okay. You can make it. Find a lobby or a hotel where someone can call you a cab.

I don't see any lobbies or hotels. Beyond my limit, I talk myself into walking more. *You can do this! Push yourself. Don't let brain injury hold you back.*

At the bottom of the hill, only a few blocks from Patty's office, I'm feeling quite proud of myself for having walked so far. Amidst a crowd of people, at the intersection, we wait for the "Don't Walk" pedestrian signal to change. I feel lit up, enthralled by being out and free!

Leaning upon my cane, I wait among the tourists for the pedestrian crossing signal. While crossing the street my foot doesn't step onto the ground as my brain intends. I fall face-first in the middle of the street. The asphalt skins my palms, elbows, knees, and chin. People rush to help the crippled woman on the ground in the middle of the crosswalk.

I'm in a blur. A hand pulls me up.

"Are you okay?"

I nod my head and walk, as evenly as possible, to the safety of the sidewalk. Once I am leaning against the security of the immovable building, I utter, "Thank you."

Another person asks, "Do you need help?"

"I'll be fine," I say. "I just need a moment."

The crowd of people stream away.

Don't cry. Don't let them see you cry. Patty's office is only a block or so away. You can make it.

Upon seeing me, Patty, aghast and concerned, immediately demands, "What happened?!"

"I fell."

"Are you alright?" she asks, although I know that she knows I'm not.

"Yeah. Let me wash myself up."

In the bathroom, I pick out the gravel from my scrapes and dab them clean with soap and paper towels. In this moment, I'm most upset about ruining the black tights that I wear under my just-below-the-knee-length black skirt. *That's just weird, Fado. All of the complicated layers of experiencing today and being hurt, and you're worried about a pair of eight-dollar tights?* Maybe it's my mind's way of distracting me from the fallout of a huge day.

Patty has set up a bed for me on the floor of her office. I lie down and quiet the screeching buzzsaw-like energy in my head until it succumbs to a honeybee-drone. Sleep doesn't come. But I know that keeping still will help.

After an hour of lying down, I don't feel ready to get up, but I convince myself otherwise. *I just want to be home.* The subway will whisk me home quickly, in less than a twenty-minute ride. *Just do it, Fado.*

Mishaps snowball. After only a few more, Hubert and the girls pick me up from the BART station and drive me home. I don't take time to chat. I go straight to bed. In silence I lie in wait for the fractured pieces of my day to float back into place.

When I think of the lawsuit, I think of that fall in the street of San Francisco.

If it were the case that the restaurant hired an architect, worked with building inspectors, and did nothing wrong in the remodel; if it were the case that the building inspectors did nothing wrong because the problem was latent, underneath the surface, and not observable; if it were the case that the construction company did something wrong, they would be off the hook, because in the State of Nevada there is a statute of limitations of eight years for construction liability for personal injury. In California personal injury is excluded from the construction statute of limitations liability, but not in Nevada. The remodel of the restaurant in the casino happened eight years and six months before my accident. If our case were to go to trial, and let's say, the jury awarded me a million dollars for damages and found the construction company to be the only party at fault, the judge would then announce that by virtue of the statute of limitations, the construction company pays nothing. The jury would not be informed of the statute of limitations until after the verdict because such information would skew determination of fault. My attorney kept the lawsuit active by questioning the date of the restaurant remodel. It's my impression that in the State of Nevada, the standards of justice have been stacked in favor of big business and protecting the casino industry from tourists.

We come to a settlement that nobody was at fault and receive an amount commensurate to what it would cost the defense to go to trial—just enough money to pay the medical bills remaining on our credit cards and third party liens. That's it. Case closed. Without liability, it's as if a tree fell on me in the forest, and there was no one there to witness.

Under the pressures of the lawsuit, my headache rears up into what felt like a blustering lightning storm. Stress makes my headaches worse. Losing sleep makes my headaches worse. Moving around and turning my head makes my headaches worse. Worrying makes my headaches worse. Months of legal procedures are a weather system for the perfect storm.

Asking God for help to get me through this, I paint my prayer about the storm in my head.

In the garage, I sit on a paint-splattered metal folding chair and stare at the eighteen by twenty-four inch blank canvas on the easel.

I don't even know what to paint. At a loss, I pray, *Lord Jesus, how do I get through this mess?*

As if a warming oven were turned on in my solar plexus, a sunshine glow spreads outward throughout my body. I am one-hundred-percent certain that I feel these words: *In Spirit and Truth.*

Yes, Lord, I answer, affirming that I have heard him loud and clear.

So Fado, what is true?

I look at my reflection in the old dresser mirror that is leaning against the garage wall.

Truth is, there's a storm raging in my head. I will paint my head in a storm, with lightning strikes of mirror shards. As I blend the colors to match my complexion, I enter a Zen zone, a blank sacred space without turmoil.

God, please help me through this storm.

Each day for many days I spend an hour in the garage painting, looking closely at the contours of my face, the slope of my cheeks, the set of my eyes, the pudge of my nose, trying to paint what I see. As I study and paint my image, I look more closely at the mess of the lawsuit, too.

What is true?

This is a financial disaster.

With a wash of shivers, I feel God's answer: *So what? I am the God of hope and restoration. I will see you through this.*

As if on cue in a musical presentation of my dialogue with God, the song, "Through it All," by Andraé Crouch and the Disciples plays on my cassette tape player. The song reminds me that through all of my tribulations I've learned to trust in Jesus. I sing along with gusto. The vibration of the sound resonates in my head, and I feel hopeful.

The truth of the financial disaster doesn't feel untenable when I trust in God. *Look more closely. What is true?*

It's not fair!

My protest reminds me of a five year old whining in a play yard scuffle.

As I paint the nose on the self portrait, I examine why my nose is so bent out of shape over the injustice of it all.

God places a question in my mind. *Have I ever promised you that life would be fair?*

No.

Children of God, the masses of people residing on the planet earth, not many of them encounter justice: far less than one percent. Why should I expect to stand with the privileged? It feels more authentic and organic to stand alongside the overwhelming masses who live with injustice. *Is it my national identity, class and status that expect the merit of my case to be awarded with justice?*

Yes. However, God assures me, *My love for you far exceeds any measure of fairness.*

Again, the music cues an elaborate production that dovetails with my inner dialogue with God. On the same album, *The Best of Andraé Crouch and the Disciples,* the song, "Take Me Back," plays and transports me back to the place where I first received my call to ministry: in the High Sierras above the timberline, where a small flower bloomed in a small crevice of a granite mountaintop. The memory brings joy to water my eyes with tears.

This lawsuit is above the timberline, where trees cannot

grow, situated where justice rarely takes root. Jesus endured a sham of a trial that resulted in his death on a cross. The monumental power of God's love was proven when he rose on the third day. Love beyond measure won. Death could not contain him. I believe this to be true.

Jesus, you know the way. Show me how to bloom in this rock-hard circumstance.

Almost finished. *Finally.* I've spent days upon days fiddling with the shape of my image in paint as well as mining through my thoughts about the storm of the lawsuit. Today I'll add some minor finishing touches to the painting. *I hate that there's a storm in my head.*

Outside, a storm rages. With such a torrential downpour, I open the garage door so that I can hear and see and smell the rain. Today I don't play an inspirational cassette in the boombox. Instead I listen to the music of the rain, the perfect accompaniment to finishing the painting I have decided to call *HeadStorm.* Enmeshed with the sunset sky, the self portrait is formed of menacing storm clouds. Lightning strike mirror shards are glued onto the canvas where my pain is the worst, in my neck, left side, and back of my head.

I blow out, expelling the stress and state of my pain, and then suck in air, gulping the freshness of God's living breath. Closing my eyes and mouth, I breathe in more gently through my nostrils. The stormy, ionized air smells fresh. With a deeper, fuller expanse of breath, I exhale. As my chest and diaphragm expand more, so does my consciousness. My thoughts do not expand, rather an expanding empty space with the ease and flow of a lapping stream settles within me.

Create a clean heart for me, God;
put a new, faithful spirit deep inside me!
Psalm 51:10 (CEB)

My entire being is a drop of water in the ocean depths of quietude. Eyes closed, seated in front of the easel, my mind and body are on pause for perhaps five minutes, perhaps twenty minutes; I'm not sure, because time is a construct that is absent from this incredible, uncanny sacred space. *Lead me, Holy Spirit.*

When I open my eyes, I see the painting with new eyes. The menacing clouds need to be darkened. Raindrops need to be added in with the tiniest of liner brushes. Quickly, so as not to lose the clarity of my inspiration, I thin down some Paynes Gray with turpentine and apply a glaze of nebulous shadow to my hair and around the lightening-strike-broken mirrors.

I watch in horror as a small channel of paint drips down the face of my self portrait.

No! Instantaneously, I try to rescue the painting by

grabbing a paper towel and blotting the drip and puddly clouds. But the damage cannot be undone. The veinlike path of the turpentine has erased everything beneath it. *Oh my God, it's ruined!*

A steamroller of ruination flattens me. The lawsuit, justice dismissed, chronic pain, and storm in my head are all too heavy, and the wrecked painting speaks this truth. It seems the only way I can escape any of it at all is to shift my chair ninety degrees and face the storm outside instead of the painting. Rain pummels the cement driveway and a thunderous clap shakes my senses. The heavens seem to be as mad as I am right now. Leaning my forehead into my open palms, I bawl.

No tears left, I feel empty and numb. Like the smooth, hard glass of a window pane, inside I am transparent—there is nothing else to be seen. Inside I am slick as glass, my feelings have slipped away. Raising my head from my hands, I stare blankly at the pouring rain, angled by the wind. *Good thing the storm outside is so loud. Nobody could hear me cry.* I rarely, if ever, have cried that loud and long.

Out of my blank, glassy state, I pray, *God help me.*

Immediately, God answers my plea. I feel a heavy burgundy velvet tea-length cape with a Mandarin collar and soutache embellishment draped lovingly around my shoulders. This luxurious comfort came from God, not from within me. Snug within Her warmth, the "brushes of the Spirit" instructs me, and I intuit Her every word.

The storm in my head is like the dripping paint, stripping away pieces of me in its wake, erasing so many of my abilities.

Oh—my—God, my errant brushstrokes have served my prayerful intention to paint the truth. On a wing and a prayer, my mistakes serve God's purpose when my desire meets the desire in the heart of God. My mistake is like a single vane on the shaft of a feather. What matters is where the quill of my feather is attached. When I am seated in the Holy Spirit, traditionally pictured as a dove, my failures take flight in the Spirit's winged movement. At a level more intricate than I can imagine, the Holy Spirit works within me.

A flutter of the "brushes of the Spirit" stirs within me. She feels something like the gentle, happy, innocent pitter-patter of my preteen heart when looking at a poster of Donny Osmond in *Tiger Beat* magazine. She shows me the good in the rain. The storm is washing away the smog in the air and the smell of the asphalt of the street. The storm is giving a deep drink to every plant and tree.

Lord Jesus, thank you. My breath deepens. The tension within my shoulders relaxes. The stress of the lawsuit eases. I drink deeply of the Living Water Jesus offers me.

I turn my chair to the left and face the painting. The drip, which I saw before as ruination, now looks like a stream of rain organically pouring out of the dark clouds. This looks so much better than the rain I had planned to paint by drawing in dash lines with my liner brush. Such tedious work. I scrub in some more overly-thinned Paynes Gray and then tilt the canvas so that the rain falls at an angle, just like in the storm outside. More paint drips strip away layers of my image on canvas.

Ah ... that's it ... my painted prayer is complete.

HeadStorm

There's a storm in my head.
Pain strikes like lightning:
    colliding,
        clashing,
            battling,
                raging.
My head is heavy laden:
    dank and dark menacing clouds
        on the verge of bursting.
My skin feels vague:
    Crisp perception and sure footing
        blur into a slow moving mist.

20: The Storm of a Lawsuit

I-Me-Self-Am,
     like a cloud
         scatters,
             dissipates.
Sorrow sweeps across my sight.
     Pouring,
         releasing,
             streaming,
                drenching.
Storm Rages in my head.

Lying in meadow sun,
     I remember seeing
         faces of God in the clouds.
During an Ash Wednesday act of repentance,
     I remember hearing
         God's tears in the rain.
Riding my bicycle,
     I remember feeling
         God's touch in the breeze.
I know the image of God
     in the wind,
         the rain,
             and the clouds.
Storm is full of God's image.

When I experience myself as HeadStorm
       it is good to see God's image in me.
A storm is raging in my head,
       and God is in my head, too.
I grasp this bit of grace
       —God-In-Me—
              and hold on for dear life.

                    —Donna Fado Ivery, March 1997

Headstorm, oil and mirrors on canvas, 18×24, 1997

21: Pruning

May 1997 - November 2000

THE BACK FENCE OF THE SMALL PARSONAGE in South San Francisco overlooks Orange Memorial Park, a beautiful expanse of verdant grass and varied trees, with basketball and tennis courts, playgrounds and an indoor swimming pool. The luxury of having a backyard is real, but it's nothing pretty to look at. Penned in by a tall wooden fence, the twenty-foot deep yard has a storage shed, built-in sandbox—used by generations of cats as a litter box—uneven patio, and plants here and there. An advantage of having small yards and small homes is that young families live on this street, and their children tend to play in the front yard, not the back. They get to know each other more easily.

Doing dishes at the kitchen sink, I enjoy looking out the window, above and beyond the fence, at the stately palm trees bordering the park and our backyard fence. Tall as a three-story building, canopies of palms commingle with the clouds of the sky. Smokey grey, billowy white, or engulfed by ocean fog, the clouds drift, sometimes indiscernibly, but they are always in motion. My rehabilitation strides are becoming less like the moving clouds, and more like the tops of the palm trees beyond my grasp.

21: Pruning

My sights high, I keep on trying.

I register for a morning rehabilitation swimming class at the Orange Memorial Park pool. In the buoyancy of the water I should be able to walk and perhaps jog without the fear of falling and injuring myself. A big plus is that the pool is only a block from our house, so I can walk there and back without depending upon Hubert for a ride. I'm beyond excited to find a form of exercise that is accessible to me. I want to be stronger and do my part.

I feel like a fish out of water in the class. The only person in the class who wouldn't be labeled as "elderly," my reddish-brown hair stands out amid the gray. Canes and walkers line up alongside the railing, steps, and the lift into the pool. I can do the exercises geared to those who have suffered strokes.

After class I struggle to get out of the pool. My feet feel like they are clad in cement shoes and my legs are like rubber bands. My perception is like the yet-to-be-disclosed sentence on the board of the television gameshow, *Wheel of Fortune*: Easy to decipher when the letters are illuminated, my board is missing letters. The understanding of where my body and surroundings lie is not yet clear. I need to wait my turn. The spin of a carnival wheel, as in the game, *Wheel of Fortune*, determines how soon my perception will return.

The instructor helps me by handing me my cane and leading me to a seat. "Are you okay?" she asks.

"I'm fine. I just need to sit for awhile," I lie. Actually I am so dizzy I may vomit. I close my eyes and wait.

After five minutes, I use all of my focus to shuffle out of the pool building. The feeling in my legs has improved. Now they only feel numb and weighed down by sandbags. I watch my feet closely, directing each footfall so that I won't take a tumble. I worry that I won't be able to get myself home.

Fifty feet outside of the building, my shuffling slows to an uneasy waddle and the sandbags on my feet turn to cement. My confidence is sinking fast. Soon no amount of grit or determination or concentration is enough to move my legs. What could possibly come next? My mind races like outlandish television commercials on fast forward: I'm lying on the ground, unable to move, an ambulance is called, and I ask the EMTs not to take me to the hospital, just drop me off at home a block away; I'm sitting cross-legged on the path, sobbing into my hands, and the police are called to assist the distraught and mentally unbalanced woman; I'm standing, waiting for someone to walk within earshot of me, and finally I ask a young mother to go into recreational building and call my husband, and she ignores me as if I'm a hitchhiker.

You're being ridiculous. I change the channel, but I am frozen in fear. I can't move my legs. I can't think. I don't know what to do. My gaze fixed on my pinioned feet, I pray. *Lord Jesus, what am I going to do?*

I feel his answer. *Come, sit with me for awhile.*

21: Pruning

At the invitation of Jesus, I pause and lift my eyes. I see what I have never noticed before: a park bench to my right, not eight feet away. *But how will I get there?* I focus on breathing—inhaling love, exhaling fear, inhaling—I can't think. I'm blank, even for breath work. I let the words go and instead slow and deepen each breath. After awhile I can make it to the bench.

I sit down sideways on the bench, tucking my knees up onto the seat, resting my head on my hand, supporting my elbow on the bench back. Posed, like someone engrossed in a conversation with a friend, I visit with Jesus. Others see me alone on the bench, but I am not alone. I feel the presence of Jesus. Like a beam of light in the darkness, a breath of fresh air on a hot, muggy day, a toasty down comforter on a cold, cold night, the spiritual presence of Jesus is distinct. I don't see him as the empty space that the world sees. Next to me sits an invisible figure whose spiritual form feels like a pocket of fresher-than-fresh air radiating infrared heat.

The focus of my sharing with Jesus is not the shock and horror of not being able to work my legs. Rather, I have changed the channel to notice and receive blessings: the sky, the air, the trees, the grass, the people passing by, the spacious wonder of the world around me, and the love of Jesus that pours over me. Our time together is an oasis, like the feeling conveyed in the classic Easter hymn, "In the Garden." The writer of the song was inspired by the story of Mary Magdalene's fear and horror that the body of the Crucified Jesus was stolen from the tomb, and her joy and gladness upon meeting the Risen Lord in the garden (John 20).

I come to the garden alone
While the dew is still on the roses
And the voice I hear, falling on my ear
The Son of God discloses

And He walks with me
And He talks with me
And He tells me I am His own
And the joy we share as we tarry there
None other has ever known

He speaks and the sound of His voice
Is so sweet the birds hush their singing
And the melody that He gave to me
Within my heart is ringing

Austin Miles, 1912
In the Garden

After about thirty minutes of sitting on a park bench and visiting with Jesus, I get up and walk home. My feet are heavy, but my heart is light.

21: Pruning

After three days of bedrest to recover, I call my doctor. I'm unsettled by my new experience of not being able to move my legs. He is not surprised and assuages my fears. He tells me that clearly the class is too much for me, that overdoing will set me back, and I need to start smaller. I am to continue walking every day and carefully increase the distance every so often by a house or two. If I feel the fallout of doing too much, I've walked too far.

I turn my focus to improvement available through pain management. Hubert and I seek out a major university's Pain Management Clinic in San Francisco. After very long intake sessions, the clinic places me on a tricyclic antidepressant in a small dose in order to wash the pain receptors with serotonin so that they won't be so quick to pick up on the pain signals. I am also to stop drinking coffee or having any caffeine because this can cause terrible headaches. I will go to physical therapy for my neck injury, because this, too, can cause headaches. I will check in with the counselor specializing in pain management.

The four days of caffeine withdrawal are not so bad—just a dull, low intensity ache that does not impinge on my mobility. Caffeine is not the culprit in my chronic pain. But, if the Pain Clinic wants me off it, I'll stay off. *No big deal.*

With my necessary balancing act of staying home the day after and before going out, the Clinic demands all of my out-of-the-house days except going to church on Sunday mornings. The physical therapist shows me the proper sitting position to release neck strain. It just so happens that the only chair in the house that has the proper height of arm and neck support is the avocado green recliner—the one I always knew felt right. Referred to another physical therapist researching and teaching vestibular therapy, I go weekly to her for rehab. I learn that I keep my head stoically still because my brain doesn't track movement, and if I try to read and take steps at the same time I fall. It seems that I'm the poster child for vestibular insufficiencies and therapies. For one, I follow through on doing the rehab exercises. I'm asked to come to an evening lecture she's giving on my case, but I decline. I don't have enough up-hours in the week to handle yet another appointment, and getting around in the evenings is even more difficult.

I am referred to a brain surgeon for the half-of-a-walnut-shell lump on at the nape of my skull where the glass partition first hit me. More stress. More appointments. More transportation support from Hubert. The brain surgeon orders an MRI, which turns out to be normal.

At a brain injury conference I am encouraged to hire a professional to coordinate the many therapies required for rehabilitation, a service that medical insurance doesn't cover. We don't do it.

I bring the binder of my Painting and Poetry Journal of the first three years following my head injury to my intake counseling appointment at the clinic. The therapist points to my painting and poem, *Dancing with Pain*, and tells me, "This is the goal of where we want our patients to be, where you can live life well with the pain, but the pain is not you." I am told I will not need to go to individual therapy, but should join a support group.

I try out the brain injury support group in Millbrae, close to our home in South San Francisco. People with traumatic brain injuries, caused by encephalitis, electrocution, drowning, car accidents, dying for a few minutes, and accidents like mine gather for support. A social worker leads the group, but doesn't have the finesse to curb gushers (my name for long talkers) while the group airs their complaints. I discover a friend in the support group, and we go out together. She'd pick me up, but riding with her is horrifying, so I ask about her brain injury and driving ability. She says she knows she shouldn't be driving but can't imagine being homebound and unable to drive. We don't go out after that.

I go to an Applied Kinesiologist for chiropractic adjustments as well as homeopathic remedies. Hubert and I participate in a costly regimen of biweekly acupuncture treatments and detoxing for a year.

At the clinic I am also given trigger point injections in my upper back in an effort to reduce the headaches caused by the injury to the myofacia, the connective tissues to the neck. When the needle is inserted into my brick-hard muscle,

I scream and become so dizzy I can't sit up. One of the nurses tells me that my face has turned a definite shade of green. They move me to lie down on a gurney in the hallway and call Hubert to pick me up. I am flat on my back in bed for a week, barely able to make it to the bathroom adjacent to our bedroom.

After a time of bolstering me with the addition of the tricyclic antidepressant and the removal of caffeine, I am told to stop taking Vicodin, which can cause headaches. I barrel through the first five days of flulike withdrawal symptoms, but find that the stabbing pain in my head takes away my ability to walk steadily and communicate. I can rarely understand what people say to me. I can rarely walk through the house without bumping into walls and doors. I can no longer fix my girls' lunches because my hand-eye coordination is so stilted.

Piercing pain is completely different than the headaches and bodyaches caused by narcotic or caffeine withdrawal. *I can certainly tell the difference.* After two weeks of merged, washed-out days curled up in bed, unable to even watch television, I phone the clinic and ask to speak to my neurologist. I receive a brand new piece of information: She is no longer with them. I will need to wait for an appointment and relay my entire brain injury saga to a new neurologist. Making the phone call is beyond difficult with my stabbing pain, and the prospect of talking to a new doctor for an hour seems impossible. In tears I insist that a doctor call me. Another neurologist phones me and tells me to stay the course because narcotic withdrawal can cause immobilizing pain and last for a few months. I remain resolute for a third week, and when scraping bottom, I finally phone my always helpful physiatrist/rehab physician.

He is mad. "Why are they jerking you around?" he protests.

I fill him in on the details and conclude, "It's because to be healthier, I need to get off of the narcotics. They say this pain is withdrawal and will pass."

"If you didn't have pain, would you take the pills?"

"Absolutely not," I reply with conviction. I don't even have to think about my answer, it is so obvious.

"You have a traumatic brain injury that often causes extreme headaches. You are not abusing the medicine. That's what it's for."

I resume taking Vicodin in the exact amounts and time prescribed by my doctor, and within a few hours the intensity of the pain which made it difficult for me to walk and talk and stand has abated just enough so that I am able to enjoy my young children.

For two years we seek out, try, and follow through with a number of therapies. And yet the baseline of my disabilities remains unchanged despite my commitment to rehabilitation exercises. It seems that every therapy is too tall an order to make any difference. Now five years post-injury, a plateau is normal. My walking and standing have improved. With a cane I am able to walk three blocks and stand for fifteen minutes before toppling.

In one way, reaching the plateau feels like the freedom and accomplishment of graduating from a five year Ph.D program. I've been like a full time student, investing my up hours into attending two classes/therapies every week, researching treatments, completing homework, and developing my own thesis, my own authority. In another way, reaching the plateau on my healing journey feels like I'm stuck with carrying a heavy backpack filled with the stones of disappointment.

Don't get discouraged. Theologically, I know that God makes a way out of no way. Spiritually, I feel the promise of restoration—maybe invisible to the naked eye, but it's there—behind the veil. I need to trust in the Spirit who knows how to create anew.

Doing dishes, looking up and out the kitchen window to greet the sky and the clouds and the palm trees, I am alarmed. A plume of smoke is rising out of the top of the palm tree, snaking its way up into the sky.

21: Pruning

Is the palm tree really on fire?
Can't be.

Who would have done such a thing? I imagine drunk teenagers shimmying up the three-story tall tree and lighting it on fire.

Makes no sense. Impossible.

Then the adjacent palm tree begins to smoke, too. Orange-red licks of flames appear. I phone the fire department. A flurry of sirens sound and firetrucks arrive soon after. A flock of kids gather in our backyard to watch. It's quite a show. The ladder truck extends to the top of the tree, and fire fighters scale its heights.

A neighbor tells me that this happens every so often. The palm trees are too tall for people to prune safely. Over the years of build-up, the dead-dried leaves become impacted, heat up, and self-combust. These tall mature palm trees self-prune to grow.

My recovery is like the heights of the palm tree. The tried-and-true ways of pruning for growth are like the many therapies and approaches to heal my brain injury. Pruning works best when the injury is young, and I missed the first nine months of rehab. But now my injury is older and the medically established approaches for recovery no longer reach the top.

The flaming palm trees give me hope. New growth is possible because the towering, older palm was created by

God to self-prune. My healing journey will continue beyond the efficacy of medical intervention, beyond what is common knowledge and expectation, because my body was created by God to heal itself.

I will give thanks to You,
for I am fearfully and wonderfully made.
Wonderful are Your works,
And my soul knows it very well.

Psalm 139:14 (ESV)

21: Pruning

Hubert, Aisha, Donna, and Imani Ivery, 1998

22: Finding Balance
January 1999 - August 2002

WITHIN THE FREEDOM OF MY REHABILITATION plateau, the pressure of working, working, working to improve my disabilities fades away. My new focus is making the best of what I have. It's like playing poker without a full hand, and I don't enjoy gambling.

I have a whopping two good hours at the beginning of each day when my thinking feels "normal." Stabbing pain in my head cuts me off when I overdo, and my ability to speak, read, think, walk, and understand floats away. My doctor and I pay close attention to when I need to increase my narcotic pain pills as my body builds up a tolerance. Our goal is to use the tool of only enough pain meds to get around, not to remove the pain. I would never, ever, take more than prescribed; that's a gamble I'm not willing to take. Keeping in rhythm with pain, keeping in rhythm with the hour or so respite I have with pain relievers, is the game I play.

Every single day, without exception, it's game on. Counting cards, I strategize hours and activities using the hand that I've been dealt.

- If I cook a simple dinner at lunchtime, then I can take a nap afterwards so that I can visit with Aisha and Imani when they come home from school.
- If I pay bills later than the first hour of the day, then I make errors writing the check or envelope.
- If I dial the phone in the afternoon, then I usually dial the wrong number.
- If I go to evening choir rehearsal, then I must stay in bed the entirety of the afternoon.
- If I move my head or eyes from side-to-side, then I must go to bed and keep my head perfectly still or keep my eyes closed to recuperate.
- If I walk without my cane, then my feet feel like cement and I shuffle.
- If I walk too far, then my world goes sideways.

If, then ... if then ... if then. I can't seem to win with the hand I've been dealt.

We move across the San Francisco Bay to El Cerrito where Hubert is assigned to pastor the El Cerrito United Methodist Church, near Berkeley. The church is a great place to raise children, and the parsonage is more than twice the size of the one in South San Francisco. With Imani in the first grade and Aisha in the fifth, it's perfect timing to move to a larger home.

In El Cerrito we live two blocks from the elementary school and eight blocks from San Pablo Avenue, the main street complete with businesses, restaurants, grocery store, drug store, and more. We invest in a mobility scooter so that I can get out and around without relying on Hubert for a ride to everywhere and for everything.

Freedom! The thrill I feel when driving the cherry-red scooter is as if I were driving a sports car. *Independence!* I can leave the house on my own. I can drive fast, with a breeze against my face, like I did as a toddler, reconnecting to a part of who I am. "Toodling," as I call driving the scooter, is much faster than walking ever-so-carefully with a cane. With the scooter, I can make decisions in the grocery store because the brain drain of walking doesn't usurp my focus. I can take Imani the two blocks to school without lying down for an hour afterwards to recuperate from walking. She loves to sit on my lap and drive. I can help Imani learn to ride a two-wheeler bicycle without training wheels, holding onto her hand and driving my scooter alongside her tentatively wobbling on the bike. I can browse at the clothing store because I don't need to find a place to sit down after standing for fifteen minutes. I can better manage without Hubert so he is freed up to go out of town on business. As primary caregiver, Hubert has bypassed too many continuing education opportunities. *Alleluia! No longer!*

The addition of a wheelchair has not decreased my

walking each day. Rather, it has increased my choices and uptime. My life is vastly improved.

I'm excited to attend the Annual Conference Session of the United Methodist Church. I've been attending yearly since I was sixteen years old. For four days, over a thousand clergy and laity from California and Nevada gather for worship, business, and fellowship—and lots of walking, standing and visiting. With my scooter I will be able to attend more hours and participate in more conversations.

At the conference, a colleague bends down to give me a hug and whispers into my ear, "Donna, I'm so sorry to see that you've taken to a chair."

Oh, my God. Is that what people think when they see me? A flush of shame rises in my cheeks. I am embarrassed that I appear to have worsened or given up on my healing journey. Nothing is further from the truth.

Another greets me. "Hi, Donna! So good to see you. How exciting that you have a scooter!"

"Yes!" I reply with too much gusto. My relief at having somebody see my scooter as a positive addition to my life translates into a stronger-than-usual energy and volume of my voice.

She seems not to notice. "I have a friend who got a wheelchair, and it opened up the world to her."

"Um hmm," I say, smiling, trying not to nod my head so that my headache won't become so extreme.

"Will you be at the clergywomen's luncheon?"

"Yes, I will. This year I'll be able to enjoy it so much more now that I have the scooter."

"Great. See you there!"

Those who look startled and askance at me in my scooter bother me. *Keep it true,* I tell myself. Clinging to what is true helps falseness to flake away. But it still itches.

Doing laundry is even more of a problem than ever before because in the El Cerrito parsonage the washer and dryer are downstairs. We resolve the burden of hauling laundry baskets down the steep staircase by sending them sledding down. We handle the danger of my climbing the stairs alone by putting my Nana's hand-me-down twin bed in the rumpus room downstairs. I adopt the rumpus room as my painting and daytime resting space and only climb the stairs once a day. Still, it's not enough.

I bark at Hubert, Aisha, and Imani for not putting their clean clothes away, getting them mixed up with dirty clothes, and leaving their dirty clothes on the floor. I feel as though they are intentionally making my difficult task harder, which is not true. I use a ratcheted-reaching-tool to pick up clothes off of the floor without bending over, but I inevitably set it down and cannot remember where. It's unfair. My anger spills over ... too often.

We see a marriage counselor for help.

"Why can't everyone do their own laundry?" she asks.

"The thought never crossed my mind," I say. "My mother always did the laundry for the family." The notion that I am less than I should be as a mother cuts deeply. My stomach is doing flip-flops and my body tenses.

"I'd be willing to do my own laundry," Hubert says.

"Don't you think Imani is too young to do her own laundry?" I ask. "She is only six years old." *There must be a way to resolve this issue that does not shortchange my daughters.*

Together we unpack my assumptions and weigh my needs and the needs of my family. I dole out too many negative emotions when under the stress of doing the family laundry. I conclude, "Okay, let's give it a try. Everybody does their own laundry."

"See how it goes," the therapist says, "and we'll revisit this in our next session."

The change to everyone's being responsible for their own laundry happens seamlessly. I tape a sign onto the wall of the laundry room that says, "Whites—Hot, Mediums—Warm,

Darks—Cold." I put a piece of blue tape on the washer and dryer dials to mark the most-used settings. Imani is quite pleased that she is able to do an "adult chore." Nine-year-old Aisha takes care of her laundry without grumbling. Hubert does his laundry without fanfare.

It seems that I am the only one in the house who has found laundry to be a heavy load to bear. I feel responsible for the consternation and chaos I've added to our family.

I take it to the Lord in prayer: *Jesus, forgive me.*

I feel refreshed to have my sins washed away.

Resolving the laundry problem emboldens me to make other changes. I become fastidious in my keeping in rhythm with pain, keeping in rhythm with meds, and reducing whatever causes me to wear out quickly. I become increasingly hard-lined and intractable. But my attempt to live with even more boundaries causes me more stress. The pressure is too much.

I feel an urgent longing to let it all go. I remember God's plumb line, which gave the figures a sense of gravity in my painting, *Dancing with Pain.* God's plumb line is what keeps me from falling over and I need to find balance *now.* In my devotional journal, I sketch a simplified picture of me clinging to a plumb line with my legs, letting go with my arms, swinging with the movement of wherever the breeze and sway take me. With my black pen I color around the image of my legs so that they can be seen, and the weight at the base of the plumb line appears. The "brushes of the Spirit," has made the plumb bob appear distinctly as an anchor.

The tension I hold in my body releases. My sense of being tossed about by demands settles. The strength of my

Finding Balance
    A poem discerned while drawing

Letting go,
   ~swinging~
     atop the plumb line
      God provides,
I discover the impossible—
a well-grounded anchor.

—*Donna Fado Ivery, 2000*

Finding Balance, pen on paper, 8x10, 2000

289

soul deepens. I feel the presence of Jesus, the anchor of my soul.

This hope is like a firm and steady anchor for our souls. In fact, hope reaches behind the curtain and into the most holy place.
Hebrews 6:19 (CEV)

In the most holy place of my being, the inner sanctum of my soul, I bask in God's own being. A cascade of light and energy washes over me and I feel gloriously uplifted. I know instantly how to meet needs and expectations where the bridge between has been damaged: I cannot do it. God can.

Each morning in my prayer journal, I write out pressing concerns and meditations and ask that the Holy Spirit be the manager of my day. I discover again and again that She does a better job than I could ever do:

- I need eighty dollars worth of art supplies and don't have the money in my business account to buy them. That week I receive just enough *Scarf of Tears* orders so that I can buy the supplies.
- I need to phone someone who offered to help me on an art project nine months ago. I don't have her number, and I have difficulty dialing the phone. She calls me that very afternoon.

- My dentist's receptionist asks me to come in today rather than tomorrow for my appointment. I've already lined up a ride with Hubert for tomorrow as well as planned my necessary rest times in order to go. Hubert can take me today, so I go. A pastoral emergency comes up that would have prevented him from taking me the next day.
- Editing *Voices and Silences,* the clergywomen's quarterly newsletter, I line up writers a year in advance. The week of the deadline, each writer drops the ball. Unsolicited articles arrive, and the edition is wonderfully full in depth of theme, length, and content. I could not have planned better.

I remain an overachiever with perfectionistic tendencies, but relying on the Holy Spirit makes an outcome beyond what is seemed possible. I have moved through this life as if its foundation is a simple equation of logic: to work harder plus find a way to do better equals everything will work out. I have assumed that the inverse is also true: to work less plus not do better equals everything will fall apart. This logic is famously untrue. Things fall apart and yet get better. Working less can bring about doing better. Things don't work out and yet fall into place. The true foundation of life is the *a priori* intention of God Most Holy, behind the veil, who changes the equation and all possibility.

23: Morning Star Rising
August 2002 - August 2004

WE ARE SO EXCITED. We are taking a family trip of a lifetime: a four-day Disney Cruise to the Bahamas. The *only* family vacation destination where a wheelchair is not a problem, Disney bears the golden glove of hospitality with accessibility. The norm is aisles and product placement that bar wheelchair access, unstaffed lifts and locked alternate entries, and wheelchair seating limited to one companion so that the family must split-up. Not at Disney, so we bought into the Disney Vacation Club. The buy-in bonus is a Disney Cruise. We are beyond thrilled.

Yet even the company with a great reputation for accessibility has its problems. I planned our trip using the published points and prices for a family of four in the bottom tier single stateroom. But when I call to make our reservation I am told that the accessible stateroom will not fit a family of four and therefore I will need to reserve and pay for an additional room. Hubert and I will not be able to sleep together because Aisha and Imani, ages ten and thirteen, must have an adult in their room. We cannot afford the additional room cost. I call Disney Customer Service and raise the issue of the Americans with Disabilities Act and that it's illegal to charge a family of four with a wheelchair more than a family of four without one. They are unaccommodating.

I could file a complaint, but that will take at least two weeks of my limited focus time to write the initial letter. To negotiate my up-hours, I don't shower the same day I go out and I don't go out of the house more than every other day. Hubert carries the burden of caregiving for church and home on his broad, strong shoulders. Neither of us have the additional energy needed to write a letter of complaint. I assume that families like us who manage the extra work disabilities require also do not have resources to fight the system and suffer inaccessibility in silence.

Disability is expensive and unfair. That's just the way it is.

On the phone with Mahz, I share my consternation over inaccessibility with the company with the best accessibility.

After a full measure of listening, Mahz offers, "Fado, I'd love to go on a Disney Cruise with you!"

"Are you sure?"

"You know I love Disney," she says. Mahz finds joy in the enchantment of Disney, and she is the enchanter of children. Mahz flew from Massachusetts to California to help me with each of my newborn daughters. After my accident, she visited us for a week each year and completed our income taxes.

She brings with her the treat of storytelling, whispered secrets, playing games, and doing whatever interests the girls. When she visits, the girls schedule "who gets to sleep with Mahzy."

I am so moved, my eyes brim with tears.

"You really want to pay your way and share a room with Aisha and Imani?" I ask.

"You know I do, Fado!"

Thank you, God, for Mahz.

We have planned ahead for my vacation rest schedule: Friday travel, Saturday rest, Sunday embark on the Disney Cruise. We arrive in Fort Lauderdale on Friday, check-in at a local timeshare condominium, and pick-up Chinese takeout for dinner. If we attend a two-hour-promotional spiel we can stay for two nights free. The Chinese food tastes peculiar but I chalk it up to my being spoiled by West Coast authentic Chinese cuisine. Within a few hours, all signs point to my having eaten spoiled food.

After a sleepless night of vomiting, diarrhea and dry heaves, Hubert takes me to Emergency. Mahz remains at the condo with the girls. IV fluids and anti-nausea medicine help me feel better. The doctor diagnoses diverticulitis and likely food poisoning. Because there is blood in my stool and vomit, I must follow-up with my primary physician at home and have a colonoscopy. The good news is that I can go on the cruise tomorrow as long as I rest, take antibiotics, and stick to a clear broth and soft foods diet.

Returning to the condo, I crawl into bed, curl up into a ball, and hold on tight. I feel wrung out. I'm drained emotionally, exhausted physically, and blurred mentally. I'm disappointed that I am in a weakened state for "the trip of a lifetime." I'm disappointed that I won't be able to eat many of the foods on the cruise. I'm disappointed that we will have to pay for the timeshare condo because we did not attend the sales promo while we were at the hospital this morning (the proof of ER records was not a legitimate excuse, so we must write a letter). I'm disappointed that we must pay extra for the cruise because I use a wheelchair. Another, another, another, and yet another disappointment. Pummeled by disappointment, I try to pray about it but can't find the words. Instead I simplify and ask, *Lord, help me,* and fall into a deep sleep.

The next morning we pack, rush, and embark on the cruise. As we enter the ship, our family name is announced over the loudspeaker, like announcing each guest at Cinderella's Royal Ball. The magic is cast, and we are swept up in excitement. I am glad to be here. We enjoy the musicals, characters, fireworks, movies, restaurants, pool, beach and being together. I take two long naps a day and rely upon complimentary room service to bring me soft foods. The mixture of being entertained and pampered makes this a restful and relaxing and joyous vacation.

Disney Family Vacation
Mahz, Aisha, Hubert, Don Fado, Jean Fado, Donna, and Imani

Back at home, although I feel perfectly normal, I follow-up with my primary physician as directed. She informs me that the standard of care is that a woman have a colonoscopy at age fifty, but I will need to have one now, at age forty-one, because of my now-resolved symptoms and diverticulitis diagnosis. I dutifully have a colonoscopy.

A week later, I receive a telephone call from the gastroenterologist. Evenings are the time of day when words drift in slowly, and I strain to understand. He says, "Mrs. Ivery. I'm calling to give you the results of your colonoscopy."

"Yes, doctor. Thank you for calling," I answer courteously. My brain is operating like a hovercraft with a cushion of air propelling me to skirt above the surface of my reality. I'm not really connecting to what is being said.

The doctor continues, "We didn't see any sign of diverticulitis."

"That's good," I reply.

"But we did find a five-to-seven-centimeter lipoma, and the biopsy is positive."

I feel as if as if I am sitting in a quiet worship service and someone screamed. Shivers of adrenalin course through my body.

Hubert is in an evening meeting at the church so I need to pull myself together and manage this phone call on my own. I pour my energy into annunciating clearly into this all-of-a-sudden murky consultation. "Doctor, would you please hold on for a moment so that I can write this down?"

"Of course."

I sit down at the desk, ready for hard work. I grab a used-white envelope from the recycle bag to write on and grasp the pen tightly to steady my trembling hand. I say, "Okay. I'm ready."

The doctor continues matter-of-factly. "It's a carcinoid tumor, and you'll need to see a colorectal surgeon to have it removed."

"I have a brain injury and words are slow for me right now. Would you mind repeating this?" I ask.

In a pace that allows me to wade through the murky waters, he describes again the cancerous tumor and concludes, "I want you to see a colorectal surgeon and have a body scan."

I write that down, too.

The call ends with my saying, "Thank you, doctor," but I don't know where my voice is coming from. I've put on waterproof fishing waders. I'm standing in sinking mud within a river of icy-cold-waters. I don't feel a thing.

Within two weeks Hubert and I consult with a colorectal surgeon. In an old fashioned office with tall stacks of papers, he sits behind his desk and seeks to allay our fears. "Lots of people have carcinoids. They are slow growing and don't spread until they're large. They grow about one-to-two centimeters every ten years so we just leave them in. It would be highly unusual for someone your age to have a carcinoid big enough that it must be surgically removed. You may not need surgery at all. Let me take a look to make sure."

With an invasive scope in the examination room he inspects the tumor and says, "Yep. It needs to come out."

My lipoma is the size that carcinoids spread. *Oh dear.*

He quizzes me on symptoms of a metastatic carcinoid. "Do you have any wheezing?" he asks.

"Yes. When I get bronchitis. Lots of people in my family develop asthma when they get older."

"Do you get hot or flushed?"

"Yes. But I thought that's because I'm pre-menopausal."

The surgeon explains, "Because carcinoids emit hormones, symptoms of a metastatic carcinoid can resemble menopause."

"I would never think getting hot and flushed is anything out of the ordinary," I say.

"Do you get severe diarrhea?" he probes.

"Yes. In Florida. I was doubled over and so sick that I went to Emergency. I thought it was food poisoning." My "worst luck ever" food poisoning is a harbinger of the "best luck ever" early detection of cancer.

Did we find it early enough? Foreboding fear weighs me down. My shoulders slump under the pressure.

My scans show no undetected cancer. The cancer has not spread. *Good news.*

During the surgery I wake up. I hear music. I hear casual conversation. It feels as if the surgeon is yanking my sutures so hard that my hips pull up and off the operating table and then slam down again. I am startled by the sound of banging on the operating table.

I call out, "I'm awake."

A masked medical professional leans over me, and catches my eye. "Hello, there." he says.

"Can you give me something so I can sleep?" I ask.

The anesthesiologist replies, "Donna, we can't do that. Your vitals won't allow it." Although the epidural keeps me from feeling the midsection of my body, I am fully alert to everything else, particularly the tugging and yanking.

From somewhere behind me a reassuring voice says. "We're taking good care of you."

The colorectal surgeon calls to me from beyond. "Everything's going well. I'm almost finished."

Under bright white lights in a sterile room I sense sounds and vibrations alien to my experience. I'm awake because part of me is used to being asleep. Opioid treatment of my chronic pain syndrome for years has caused part of my being to sleep through the grip of pain. My pain receptors remain on full alert and haven't had a rest for nine years. My dentist administers a few extra shots of Novocaine to deaden my nerves. Because it takes so much more to sedate me in my already partially sedated state, I was also awake for much of my colonoscopy. Chronic pain is a slippery slope.

Awake or asleep, I inhale the Breath of God, exhale what my body and mind no longer need, and wait.

Because the colorectal surgeon can visually inspect the surgery site and reoccurrence with a proctoscope, I do not need radiation. My follow-up will entail lots of colon cleansing, rectal exams, and a schedule of colonoscopies. According to the medical professionals, the scare is over.

After three months of recovery, I am physically healed, but my baseline energy has not returned. I feel slow, as if I am wearing a hazmat suit to trudge through muck and mire. My baseline-up-hours—ninety-minutes up for every hour down—has reduced to thirty-minutes up for every hour down. I can tell because when my brain-energy tank is low I drop things, bump into doorways, and put away glasses in the canned-foods cupboard. When it is time for me to rest, our cat, Mickey, meows and leads me down the long hallway into the master bedroom and into bed. The quality time I can spend with Aisha and Imani continues to be sacrificed. I visit my therapist regularly for emotional self-care.

Six months after my surgery, I have not yet rebounded.

Perhaps because I already carry a full load of brain injury disabilities, the extra load of cancer is just *too much*.

A kind woman in church says to me, "God never gives you more than you can handle."

In my head, I answer, *God help me. Too much can be plain too much.* Jesus, who knows the scourge of suffering knows when too much is too much. However, I smile and answer, "God is good."

There seems to be an impenetrable barrier preventing my deepest self from feeling God. I cannot reach silence. I cannot sense the movement of the Spirit. I feel grateful for the food poisoning, even for what I thought had been the worst luck and worst timing possible because it raised the cancer alarm. It ended up actually being a stroke of the best luck and best timing possible, still the totality of my energy is spent going through the motions of everyday living and lying down to recover. *When, O Lord? When will there be a shift? When will I regain the ground of recovery that I've spent nine too-long years to build?*

God has a long-term perspective filled with possibility that I cannot even imagine. Wading through the "ugh," I yearn to consult with God, Jesus, and the Holy Spirit, but feel numb.

How can I break through the barrier? In the past, painting

my prayers helped. Very aware that I have not yet bounced back, Mom and Dad offer to host me for a week-long painting retreat. They have just removed all of the equipment out of the workshop in their backyard and plan to convert the room to a studio apartment. The walls are freshly painted, but the cement floors do not yet have carpet. They would put a twin bed in the workshop, tarp everything except the floors—walls, bed, student desk, and boombox—feed me, and leave me alone. *Perfect.* I look forward to my painting retreat and feeling better.

Hubert loads our eight-by-four-foot pull-trailer with a mass of canvases and oil painting supplies and delivers me to Mom and Dad's. After I sleep a few hours to recuperate from the ninety-minute drive, Dad helps me to set up my painting table and easel.

On the first day of my painting retreat, I set up the room to be a studio so that when I again feel the "brushes of the Spirit" I'll be ready to paint.

The simple steps of setting out the tubes of oil paints, jars of odor-free turpentine, paper palette, canvases and brushes, are satisfying to me, like a meditative practice, something like walking a labyrinth—which I used to be able to do but can no longer. Watching my feet, walking inward and outward, focusing on the mundane, I sometimes reached spiritual center.

I pray, *Lead me, Lord. Show me the way to recover,* and promptly fall asleep.

Rising from bed, I walk the eight feet to my folks' house to eat, return to the studio, and pray. *Lead me, Lord. Show me the way to recover.* Allowing these words to linger, I again fall asleep.

Eat, pray, sleep. Eat, pray, sleep.

On the second day of my painting retreat, I deepen my breath-work, quiet my mind, focus on inhaling the positive and exhaling the negative, inhaling the presence and power of the Holy Spirit, exhaling conscious and subconscious disconnection.

And I fall asleep.

The order of my day remains firm: Eat, pray, sleep. Eat, pray, sleep. Eat, pray, sleep.

On the third day of my painting retreat, I am able to remain awake for about twenty minutes before drifting off to sleep. My senses and feelings feel unrooted and afloat.

I try playing a few CDs of my favorite Christian music. Usually gospel music adds a measure of joy to my heart and lifts me to dance along in my mind and in the movement of my paintbrush. But not now. The words seemed to clutter my sacred space. I switch to instrumental music, and this, too, feels like an interruption save one composition, a compilation of two songs, "On Eagle's Wings" and "Wind Beneath My Wings" by Steve Hall. Played with harp, violins, wind chimes, rainstick, and piano, this song intermingles with the ebb and flow of my feelings. I set the boombox to "Repeat 1," and listen to this one song continuously.

The lyrics to "Wind Beneath My Wings" by Bette Midler and "On Eagle's Wings" by Fr. Michael Joncas scatter away like dandelion seeds carried by the wind. A few of these seeds are carried within my drifting mind and planted within my deepening breath: God bears me, supports me through it all, and Spirit, the "Breath of Dawn," initiates the yet-to-be-seen new day.

On the fourth morning of my painting retreat, I want to paint, but my desire is born out of guilt. Dad has nailed and stapled tarps to the walls of the to-be-guest cottage so that I can paint. Hubert has loaded and hauled the trailer with art supplies so that I can paint. How dare I not paint when others have given so much so that I can!

I can paint some florals. I always enjoy that. People like them.

Don't do it, Fado, I warn. You need to paint the honesty of heart so that the Spirit can lead you. Spirit and Truth are always partners.

I don't yet have a focus or an image for any painted prayer because my inner senses remain adrift. I have no idea what the truth is or why it is taking me so long to recover from the cancer that has been successfully removed.

Lord, Jesus, I am waiting on you. Lead me, I pray and fall asleep.

During the day, the medley "On Eagles' Wings/Wind Beneath My Wings" plays continuously.

On day five I awaken from a good night's sleep with an image emblazoned on my mind: a seascape with turbulent waters, moving from the dark of night to first morning light, the Holy Spirit, the "Breath of Dawn," blowing-through, ushering in a new day.

I leap out of bed to the easel, which holds a three-by four-foot canvas, primed and ready to paint. With sweeping strokes and a four-inch brush, I paint quickly to capture the vision in my sleep: the Holy Spirit in the colors of yellow and white whipping through like tongues of light, converting the night to day, the sky and seas celebrating in the brightest, happiest hues of magenta, rose, orange, purple, and Cerulean Blue. Seeing the hope and promise of a new dawn taking form in front of me, shivers of adrenalin flow. I feel a surge of energy, a natural high.

My sprint-like painting overflows onto another large canvas. Sweating, I clean my hands, eat breakfast, and lie down to rest.

On days five and six of my retreat, I paint sixteen *Breath*

Breath of Dawn, oil on canvas, 48x36, 2003

of Dawn oil paintings, from sizes five-by-seven inches to three-by-four feet.

The "brushes of the Spirit" has answered my prayer: *Lead me, Lord. Show me the way to recover.* Circadian rhythms, a process of wake and sleep, affects all of the creatures and nature of earth and sky. Physiologically and psychologically, I have been pressed to sleep in order to recover. Even when I was "supposed" to be fully awake, a different rhythm within me demanded that I rest. Spiritually, I have felt compelled to be completely still, sleep, and wait.

In the most dismal place, at the longest point of night—just before sunrise—the morning star shines its glimmer of hope.

> So *we have the prophetic word strongly confirmed.*
> *You will do well to pay attention to it, as to a lamp*
> *shining in a dismal place, until the day dawns and*
> *the morning star rises in your hearts.*
>
> 2 Peter 2:19 (HCS)

When cognition floats and I'm unable to find my way, the Holy Spirit, the "Breath of Dawn," moves and ushers in a new day. Like the Spirit of God that hovers over the face of the deep before Creation happens, the Breath of God will create, *a priori*, new possibility. The "brushes of the Spirit" lulls me to sleep and creates anew in me when the time is right. I can count on it, like I can count on the sun rising in the East.

I feel renewed, even spry. I have turned the corner in my recovery from cancer surgery.

Breaking open spiritually ushered in evidence of a new day. Within the year after my painting retreat, we buy our own home in nearby Richmond, on the flatlands and close to BART. I can drive my scooter to many more places. Hubert builds a study and studio in our backyard.

A new day has dawned.

Glad Floral, oil on canvas, 5×7×1, 2004

24: Circle Dance
July 2007

THIRTEEN YEARS AFTER MY HEAD INJURY, in the painting studio of the Richmond Art Center, I sit on the gray metal stool, rest my head against the wall behind me, and gather myself to paint.

Actually I've been gathering myself to paint for the past week. No, ever since I started painting my prayers twelve years ago, I've been gathering myself to paint. Whereas my practice of painting regularly began as a necessity to express myself after brain injury, for the last ten years or so, painting has been a way for me to play with the "brushes of the Spirit," the same Creative Spirit who is God. *Such a delight.* Color is varying lengths of refracted light. Painting for me is playing with color, playing with *"da light."*

Painting three large freeform silk paintings at a time requires disciplined pacing and set-up beforehand. After lunch I set up during Open Studio hours at the Richmond Art Center, only two blocks from our home. The necessity of a solid two-hour nap in between set-up and the 6:30 PM painting class bridges my slow-mo-evening-brain-gaps. Two three-by-two foot and one three-by-five-foot stretched silks, about twenty five-by-seven silks, jars of acrylics, disposable Costco Chicken Caesar Salad plastic bowls, a black plastic deli tray, an old whisk broom with white bristles permanently tinted like Easter eggs, a ten-gallon bucket of water, and my four-foot-long brushes are all set up to paint. The set-up hassle usurps precious creative focus time during class, so it's perfect for me that I can set up in the afternoon.

Leaning my head upon the solid wall has served to settle the sensation of churning motion, something like walking off a boat tossed by waves onto solid land. It takes awhile for the whole world to stop moving. Just walking around churns up everything. Now, settled to the point of stillness, I open my eyes and scroll through the songs on Aisha's old iPod. I'm careful not to move my head or eyes too much, since that will dishevel my perceptions. Pushing the earbuds into my ears, I focus on embracing and retaining the empty stillness in my heart and mind and pray, *Holy Spirit, lead me.*

As if the Spirit hears my question, I hear the answer as solidifying desire inside of me: "Draw the Circle Wide." It's a song by Gordon Light sung by Jim and Jean Strathdee on their album, *Stand Up for What is Right.* I know the song and musicians well. I've been listening to their albums and singing their songs in church since the 1970s.

The upbeat folk song draws an image of an ever-widening

circle of people and strums effortlessly through me. The melody, rhythm, words, guitar, and resonance of Jean and Jim's vocals roll gently along my heart and mind. I believe that both heart and mind have their own wavelength, the energy of the Spirit has Her own wavelength, and a song, too, has its own wavelength. Each wavelength, like refracted light, blends into a composition. Like color theory and music theory, how wavelengths are juxtaposed and blended creates a unique spiritual composition. Starting with the wavelength of my heart and mind by tuning it to neutral, or the center point of stillness, I can embrace more clearly the "brushes of the Spirit's" creative impulse. The song strums along in the background.

In the same breath that I reach my stillpoint, the words of the song flow, "God the still point of the circle, 'round whom all creation turns."

Yes, this is the song I will paint to tonight. I set the iPod on "Repeat One" and listen as the one song plays over and over again. I've learned through my painting life that changing the song changes the image, so it's best for me to stick to one song per painting. Shushing my figure-it-out tendencies, I keep myself open to the movement of the Spirit, my eyes closed, and my head perfectly still. After playing the song four times through, a warm sparkle of inspiration flows through me, a scintillating tingle drifts through me from the top of my head, through my body, and out the soles of my feet. The "brushes of the Spirit" has given me a vision of what to paint.

Like a surfer paddling quickly to catch the wave, I rush to not lose the inspiration, and pour out transparent magenta, yellow, and blue paint onto the large-black-plastic deli tray I pilfered from the church potluck trash. Unceremoniously with little bending over, I drop this palette onto the floor. The thicker paint is good, but I also need some that is thinned down because they both behave differently on silk. With cupped hands I ladle water from the ten-gallon bucket into pie-pan-sized salad bowls to make diluted transparent color. With quick, snapping wrist motions like flinging chicken feed, I sprinkle water onto the silk canvases on the tarp-covered floor. I need some wet silk, some dry silk, because paint behaves differently on each. Just like when I painted my prayers when words wouldn't come, and the "brushes of the Spirit" painted alongside me and completed the painting beyond my imagination, today the "brushes of the Spirit" continues to paint alongside me. Still today—when words come to me so much more easily—I continue to paint with a balance of knowing and not knowing, along with the "brushes of the Spirit." The wet spots on the silk are the spaces where I have very little control and the Spirit adds in the fullness. This truly is Spirit Brush Art.

Dipping a whisk broom into the diluted paint pan, I flick and spray paint in forms of barely discernible cloud formations.

A resounding uplifting chorus with clapping plays in my ears, as if I'm swaying along with friends singing and laughing around a campfire. I pick up my four-foot-long brush and paint in rhythm to the music. I've attached about three feet of PVC pipe to three of my paint brushes with insulating foam. This serves two purposes. One: I can paint large paintings on the floor without much bending over, and two: The long brush keeps my strokes loose and impressionistic. Matisse used long brushes. With a long brush, there isn't any way to have complete control over where the paint goes. Instead I need to dive in and swim along!

The song tells of drawing an ever-widening circle of belonging. I paint impressionistic body flairs of energy dancing in an oblong circle. I add in someone seated in a wheelchair to join in the dance. There must be a wheelchair in order to include those who dance seated. The song sings of no one standing alone. This is what Martin Luther King, Jr. called the *Beloved Community*. No one need to stand, play, or dance alone.

There must be children. There must be different hues of skin tones. I'm singing along in my mind, in the zone, blending color out of muscle memory, not thinking. I know my favorite yellow, and how when mixed with florescent magenta I get an intense, vibrant orange, and how to mix varying hues of green. In the past I've tried at least sixteen different yellows and at least a dozen oranges, and I know the select few that have wavelengths whose melody resonates with my own. One color next to another evokes a new focus, a new vibration.

My body sways. I'm dancing, painting, brushing, spraying water, flicking with the whisk broom. Twenty minutes flash by during my delightful dance with Spirit and paint.

Sit down, Fado. Leave space enough for the Spirit to do Her work.

Immediately I sit back down on the tall stool and lean the back of my head against the wall.

Good.

There are only a few puddles on the silk backed by waxy freezer paper. In silk painting all of the elements have such a delicate balance. Too much water, all of the color turns into a solid mass. Too much paint, not much color travels with the silk. Too many colors, they swirl together and turn muddy. Too thick paint, it lays atop the silk like a plastic blob. Too thin paint, it's like painting with an eraser. The delicate dance of color on the silken canvas is so similar to my healing journey. A bit of this. A bit of that. Too much head movement, and I'm down for the count. Not enough pain relievers, I'm in bed too long. Not enough horizontal resting time interspersed throughout the day, and my spatial reasoning and mental acuity take a dive. Not enough space in my days or my mind for the Spirit to move, and my fervent hope for healing is dismissed.

The Advanced Painting Class teacher, Myong Stebbins,

stops by my corner of the room to give feedback and answer questions.

Myong knows that I startle easily when I'm in deep focus, so she waves her hands to catch my eye, and asks, "Fado, how's it going?"

I pull out my earbuds and answer. "Good."

"I didn't drop by earlier because you're so into it tonight." That's a great teacher for you. Myong is dedicated to support my own artistic voice, not for me to copy her style. She takes the time to perceive what I'm about and how I'm going about painting, and she's a fantastic artist and technician.

"Um hmm," I say, careful not to nod my head because I want to reserve all head movement tonight for painting.

"I noticed how much your whole body moves when you paint. It's like you're dancing as you paint."

I smile.

"And you've got great movement in your painting, too."

Gazing at the painting, I can just now see it. "Yeah. I like that," I say, and pause to take in the painting. "Do you have any suggestions for composition?"

Myong pulls up a stool and sits down. We sit quietly, and absorb the details of the painting. Impressionist beings of varying sizes and color—purple, orange, green, yellow, pink, blue, green—dance in a widening circle.

"It's really great the way it is. Don't do much to it, Fado.

24: Circle Dance

I would suggest adding a deeper color in these two corners so that the eye goes to the circle rather than the white edges."

"I see what you mean," I say, and use my four-foot brush as a pointer. "If I add this deep orange over here, the light blue people and the other dancers will come forward."

"Yeah, that would work. But Fado, don't do too much. Leave it," she says, raising one eyebrow in admonishment and humor.

Lord knows that I've ruined many a painting by tinkering the creative pizzaz right out of it. I've been coming to Myong's class at the Richmond Art Center for about three years, long enough for her to know my growing edges.

"Thanks, Myong."

"Sure thing, Fado," she says, and then proceeds to check in with the other painters in the class.

Soon I have blended and added intense orange to a few of the corners. I like the vibrancy of the color and the circle dance movement. But I can't yet tell how the whole painting will look when it's finished. Like a small drop of water spreading lickety-split on a silk blouse, water moves and dries quickly on silk, and the diluted paint travels with the water as it dries. I won't be able to see the finished images until it's all dry.

I'm done with this painting for now, so I press the stop button on my iPod and return to the stool along the wall to rest my head, pray, and select another song to play as I paint a few more canvases.

The next morning, I return to the Painting Studio at the Richmond Art Center to pick up my dry paintings. My mouth gapes open in astonishment when I see the painting which I decided overnight to call *Circle Dance*. The "brushes of the Spirit" has completed the painting, added facial features to the figures, as well as ghost-like spirit bodies to the dance! There are so many more in the dance than I had expected, intended, or dreamed.

A phrase of the song that repeated and repeated when I painted Circle Dance comes back to me now.

> *Let the dreams we dream be larger*
> *than we've ever dreamed before.*
> *Let the dream of Christ be in us,*
> *Open every door.*
> *Words and Music by Gordon Light*
> *Draw the Circle Wide*

I am blown away. I am called back to my stillpoint, the seat of hope, and so I sit down on the tall stool and take it all in. *Circle Dance* is a happy and hopeful painting. The vibrant colors, ethereal movement, and community of people and spiritual beings move joyfully together. The "brushes of the Spirit" blows through me with a grand whoosh of happiness and hopefulness. The Spirit can complete a painting beyond my expectation, experimentation, and manipulation. This same creative Spirit can heal me, beyond my imagination. My heart overflows with praise.

Circle Dance, acrylic on silk, 54x33, 2007

You have turned for me my mourning into dancing; you have loosed my sackcloth and clothed me with gladness.   *Psalm 30:11 (ESV)*

Epilogue

AS THE SPIRIT PROMISED in my painting, *Circle Dance*, I have opened many doors and crossed many thresholds to discover healing beyond the imagination.

Now I no longer walk with a cane or use a wheelchair or have excruciating pain that requires narcotic treatment. *Alleluia*! This miracle came about through working closely with the Holy Spirit and following where She leads. Through coincidences which were answered prayers, I was led to work with a skilled spiritual healer. I tell the story of my healing beyond expectations in book two of this inspirational memoir: *Sleep, Pray, Fly: Spirit Journey to Healing*. The extraordinary tale is biblical, not traditional, and not a comfortable one for every local church. God asks me to share it and so I do.

I don't think I would have come so far in my healing journey if brain injury did not teach me to rely fully upon the Lord and to interpret the movement of the "brushes of the Spirit."

I love to preach, speak, write, paint, bake bread, and watch the sunrise. Careful pacing remains a necessity.

My family feeds me in so many ways.

I am blessed.

Acknowledgments

WRITING *Sleep, Pray, Heal: A Path to Wholeness and Well-Being* is a way for me to claim and name the miraculous healing that astounds me, to set a marker on this wild journey called life. Although I took on the task of writing this book to commemorate the twentieth anniversary of my head injury, within my disability-instituted balancing act of rest and movement, it took me about eight years to write. I could not have done so without the help of so many, most of whom are not named.

I thank God, whom I know as the Creator, Jesus Christ, and the Holy Spirit. Your presence and power has led me to dimensions beyond my imagination, to healing beyond my expectation.

I thank my husband, the Reverend Dr. Hubert Ivery. I am grateful for the depth of your spirit, towering commitment, chuckle that lightens me, and broader-than-typical shoulders upon which I lean. I love you.

I thank my daughters, Aisha and Imani Ivery. It is such a privilege to be your mother and share in your laughter, tears, and days. Nothing makes me happier than to see both of you letting your unique and special light shine.

I thank my parents, Don and Jean Fado. You have

Acknowledgements

nurtured and loved me in more ways than you know.

I thank Dr. Elizabeth Bettenhausen, my theology professor at Boston University School of Theology. Within a year both of us sustained disabling brain injuries and began an exchange that led to my "Art and Brain Injury Journal." Thank you for your friendship and stunningly clear search for meaning.

I thank my editor, Linda Watanabe McFerrin. You have encouraged and coached me to write on many levels—spiritually, cognitively, and compassionately.

I thank Pamela Feinsilber, the developmental editor of my second book, *Sleep, Pray, Fly: Spirit Journey to Healing*, which I first wrote. Your critique that I needed to write more about my injury and backstory gave rise to this book.

I thank Book Passage bookstore in Corte Madera, California. Your Path to Publishing program has assisted me to find my voice and path as author.

Thank you to those who have hosted me in their homes for my writing retreats: Jean and Dave Braun, Don and Jean Fado, Barbara and Kelly Pierce, Gretchen and Jean Dunoyer, Princess and Malcolm Campbell, Dixie and Rob Jennings-Teats, and Nancy Marsden.

Thank you to Dr. Laurie Chaikin of OptoRehab and

Cindy Gibson-Horn of Motion Therapeutics for fitting me with a BalanceWear Stabilizing Garment, which reduced my tremors enough so that I could write at my laptop.

Thank you to those who have supported me with grants to articulate my passion for the *Art of Healing*. The California Arts Council, the National Arts and Disabilities Center at the University of California Los Angeles, the California-Nevada Annual Conference of the United Methodist Church Continuing Education, Spiritual Direction, Coaching, and Supportive Services.

Thank you to the many people who have supported my crowd-funding campaign to publish and promote this book. A special shout out to my angel-level donors whose generosity fostered success: Ellie Charlton, Namnama Alberto, John and Christine Boogaert, Don and Jean Fado, David Fado, Linda Watanabe McFerrin, Catherine Braun, Lynette Grandison, Bishop Warner Brown, Dave and Jean Braun, Jill Perry, Sharon Grant, Bonnie Schell, Roger Morimoto, and Joanna Greenshields. Your support warms my heart, buoys my spirit, and makes straight in the desert a highway.

Author's Invitation and Website

You can help! Please post a review on Amazon.com, as this is the best way for independent authors to gain exposure and help sales.

Donna Fado Ivery would love to hear from you.

To contact the author, please visit her website. There, you can also sign-up to receive news about Donna's upcoming books and more.

www.DonnaFadoIvery.com
www.AdventuresInHealing.com

Instagram: DonnaFadoIvery
Facebook: Donna Fado Ivery/Author, Adventures in Healing
Twitter: @DonnaFadoIvery

References & Permissions

PART I: BREAKING OPEN

John Greenleaf Whittier, "Dear Lord and Father of Mankind," In W. Garrett Horder, editor *Congregational Hymns,* (London, 1884). The hymn was adapted from John Greenleaf Whittiier's poem, "The Brewing of Soma," published in 1872.

CHAPTER 1: FALLEN

The plate glass partition measured 58 inches by 78 inches by one-half inch thick. The weight was 207.35 pounds.

CHAPTER 2: SHADOWS OF SAINT FRANCIS

Scripture quotations are within Gratis Use copyright guidelines.

Immanuel Kant, Patricia Kitcher editor and W. Pluhar translator, *Critique of Pure Reason* (Indianapolis: Hackett. 1996). Originally published as Kritik der reinen Vernunft in 1781.

Augustine, edited and translated by Carolyn J.B. Hammond, *Confessions of Saint Augustine, Book 1,* (Cambridge, Massachusetts: Harvard University Press, 2014-2016), 67.

Augustine, Gareth B. Matthews, editor and Stephen McKenna, translator, *On the Trinity: Books 8-15,* (Cambridge, UK: Cambridge University Press, 2002), 89-90.

Paul Sabatier, *The Road to Assisi, 120th Anniversary Edition* (Paraclete Press, 2014).

Omer Englehart, *Saint Francis of Assisi*, (Chicago: The Franciscan Herald Press, 1965).

Jon Sweeney, translator, *Francis of Assisi in His Own Words* (Brewster, Massachusetts: Paraclete Press, 2018).

Anonymous, "The Prayer of Saint Francis," in La Clochette, (Paris: La Ligue de la Sainte-Messe, 1912).

Civilla D. Martin, words and Charles H. Gabriel, composer, "His Eye Is on the Sparrow" in D.B. Towner et.al., *Revival Hymns:: A Collection of New and Standard Hymns for Gospel and Social Meetings, Sunday Schools and Young People's Societies*. (Chicago: Bible Institute Colportage Association, 1905).

CHAPTER 4: A LOVE STORY

Walter Brueggemann, *The Creative Word: Canon as a Model for Biblical Education* (Fortress Press, 1982).

Dorothy Graham Gast, "Do You Remember the First Shell Homes: They were much better than two room shacks," @ www.DaysGoneBy.me, July 13, 2017. The article has photos of Alabama slave shacks and Jim Walter shell homes reminiscent of Hubert's grandparents' homes. https://daysgoneby.me/shell-homes-provided-shelter-many-south/, Accessed May 2016.

Frederick A. Norwood, *The Story of American Methodism* (Nashville: Abingdon Press, 1974).

F. R. Kluckhohn & F. L. Strodtbeck, *Variations in Value Orientations.* (Evanston, IL: Row, Peterson,1961).

CHAPTER 5: DESERT DWELLING

J. J. Bazarian, et al., "Emergency department management of mild traumatic brain injury in the USA," in Emergency Medicine Journal, 2005;22:473–477. doi: 10.1136/emj.2004.019273, https://www.ncbi.nlm.nih.gov/pmc/articles/PMC1726852/pdf/v0 22p00473.pdf, Accessed September 2018.

Cecilia Tasca, Mariangela Rapetti, Mauro Giovanni Carta, and Bianca Fadda, "Women And Hysteria In The History Of Mental Health," in Clinical Practice & Epidemiology in Mental Health, 2012, 8, 110-119. https://www.ncbi.nlm.nih.gov/pmc/articles/PMC3480686/, Accessed May 2017.

Paul Tillich, *Systematic Theology, Volume I* (Chicago: University of Chicago Press, 1951), 64.

PART II: PAINTING PRAYERS

"K" (Anonymous), "How Firm a Foundation," in John Rippon and Isaac Watts, editors, *A Selection of Hymns from the Best Authors: Intended to be an appendix to Dr. Watt's Psalms and hymns* (Burlington, New Jersey: S.C. Ustick, 1787).

CHAPTER 6: TOO DEEP FOR WORDS

Elisabeth Kübler-Ross, *The Stages of Death and Dying,* (New York: Routledge, 1969).

CHAPTER 10: ROCKING LOST

James Strong, *Strong's Exhaustive Concordance of the Bible: Updated and Expanded ed.* (Peabody, MA: Hendrickson Publications, 2012)

Jürgen Moltmann, *The Spirit of Life: A Universal Affirmation* (Minneapolis: Fortress, 1992), 157-158.

Lee Martin McDonald and James A. Sanders editors, *The Canon Debate: On the Origins and Formation of the Bible* (Peabody, Mass: Hendrickson Publishers, 2002).

Sandra Schneiders, *Women and the Word: the Gender of God in the New Testament and the Spirituality of Women,* (New York: Paulist Press, 1986).

Samuel Sebastian Wesley, "Lead Me, Lord," in Corp Authors: United Free Church of Scotland, *The Anthem Book of the United Free Church of Scotland,* (London: Novello, 1905).

CHAPTER 12: COLORING FAMILY

Marian Diamond, Arnold Scheibel, and Lawrence Elson, *The Human Brain Coloring Book*, (Oakdale: Coloring Concepts, Harper Perennial, 1985)

CHAPTER 13: HOPES DASHED

African American Spiritual, "Rock My Soul," In William Francis Allen, Charles Pickard Ware, Lucy McKim Garrison, *Slave Songs of the United States,* (A. Simpson & Co. 1867).

CHAPTER 14: BROKEN YET WHOLE

"Seasonal Affective Disorder (SAD)" www. Mayoclinic.org https://www.mayoclinic.org/diseases-conditions/seasonal-affective-disorder/symptoms-causes/syc-20364651, pg 175, Accessed March 2017.

Don Climer, "'Humus beings'—wordplay or clue to our origin?" In World Together (blog), *Mennonite World Review,* October 9, 2015, http://mennoworld.org/2015/10/19/the-world-together/humus-beings-word-play-or-clue-to-our-ori

United Methodist Church (U.S.), and Methodist Church (U.S.). "Imposition of Ashes Liturgy," in *The Book of Worship for Church and Home : With Orders of Worship, Services for the Administration of Sacraments, and Aids to Worship According to the Usages of the United Methodist Church.* (Nashville, Tennessee.: United Methodist Publishing House, 1965), 179.

James Strong, *Strong's Exhaustive Concordance of the Bible: Updated and Expanded* ed. (Peabody, MA: Hendrickson Publications, 2012).

CHAPTER 15: FORMED BY TEARS

Norman Vincent Peale, *The Power of Positive Thinking: And, the Amazing Results of Positive Thinking.* (New York: Fireside/Simon & Schuster, 2003).

Robert Harold Schuller, and Paul David Dunn. *Possibility Thinkers Bible: The New King James Version.* (Nashville: T. Nelson, 1984).

Emilie E. Godwin, PhD; Jeffrey S. Kreutzer, PhD; Juan Carlos Arango-Lasprilla, PhD; and Tara J. Lehan, PhD, "Marriage After Brain Injury: Review, Analysis, and Research Recommendation" in *Journal of Head Trauma Rehabilitation* (January/February 2011 - Volume 26 - Issue 1), pp. 43–55, doi: 10.1097/HTR.0b013e3182048f54

CHAPTER 16: BARELY THERE

Catherine Keller, "Self and God: Separation, Sexism, and Self," *In Creating Women's Theology: A Movement Engaging Process Thought*, ed. Monica Coleman, Nancy R. Howell, and Helene Tallon Russell (Eugene, Oregon: Pickwick, 2011), 85-97.

Rosemary Radford Ruether, "Rejection of Dualism" *In Creating Women's Theology: A Movement Engaging Process Thought,* ed. Monica Coleman, Nancy R. Howell, and Helene Tallon Russell (Eugene, Oregon: Pickwick, 2011), 60-70.

Dale Martin, "The Corinthian Body: Chapter 1, The Body in Greco-Roman Culture," editor Laura Laura Nasrallah, in Early Christianity: The Letters of Paul, CD, 2013. https://genius.com/Dale-martin-the-corinthian-body-chap-1-the-body-in-greco-roman-culture-annotated Accessed August 6, 2019.

James B. Nelson, *Embodiment: An Approach to Sexuality and Christian Theology*. Minneapolis: Augsburg Pub. House, 1978.

Louis William Countryman, *Dirt, Greed, and Sex : Sexual Ethics in the New Testament and Their Implications for Today*. Philadelphia: Fortress Press, 1988.

PART III: CREATING ANEW

Samuel Longfellow, "Holy Spirit, Truth Divine," in Samuel Longfellow and Samuel Johnson, editors, *Hymns of the Spirit* (Boston: Ticknor and Fields, 1864).

CHAPTER 18: WATERSHED

Jim Strathdee, words and music, "Holy Spirit, Speak for Us." (Sacramento, Caliche Records, 1997). Used with permission. www.StrathdeeMusic.com

CHAPTER 19: DANCING WITH PAIN

Jenő Barcsay, *Anatomy for the Artist*. (New York: Barnes & Noble Books, 1995)

CHAPTER 20: THE STORM OF A LAWSUIT

Andraé Crouch and the Disciples, "Through it All," and "Take Me Back" words by Andraé Crouch, *In The Best of Andrae*, (Light, LS 5678, 1975).

CHAPTER 21: PRUNING

Austin C. Miles, "In the Garden," in J. Lincoln Hall, editor et.al, *The Gospel Message No. 2*, (New York: Hall Mack Co, 1912).

CHAPTER 23: MORNING STAR RISING

Steve Hall, "On Eagle's Wings/Wind Beneath My Wings," in On Eagles' Wings, CD (CD Baby, 1996).

CHAPTER 24: CIRCLE DANCE

Jim & Jean Strathdee, "Draw the Circle Wide," words and music by Gordon Light, In *Stand Up for What is Right*, CD (Sacramento: Caliche Records, 2007) www.StrathdeeMusic.com

Gordon Light, "Draw the Circle Wide," (Common Cup Company, 1994). Used with permission. You can find Bishop Gordon Light's music at www.commoncup.com.

AWARDS

Finalist, William Faulkner-William Wisdom Creative Writing Competition 2019, Nonfiction Book category, with 209 entires from six countries competing.

Writer's Digest 2019 Award, Inspirational/Spiritual Category.

Scripture Translations

AMP: Amplified Bible

BSB: Berean Study Bible

CEB: Common English Bible

CEV: Contemporary English Version

ESV: English Standard Version

HCS: Holman Christian Standard Bible

ICD: International Children's Bible

LEB: Lexham English Bible

MSG: The Message

NIRV: New International Reader's Version

NIV: New International Version

NKJV: New King James Version

NLT: New Living Translation

NRSV: New Revised Standard Version

RSV: Revised Standard Version

VOICE: The Voice

Scripture Index

Genesis
1:1-2.............141
1:27.............20
2:7.............178
9:11-13.........146

1 Kings
12:28.............243

Job
2:13.............212

Psalms
4 & 5.............134
30:11.............319
51:10.............261
59:16b.............77
139:14.........280

Isaiah
9:6-7............. 175
43:19........... 225
55:8-9......... 141

Amos
7:8.............243

Habakkuk
2:1-3.............84

Matthew
3:16-17.........193
5:13.............193
6:34............. 26
17:20.............176
22:37-39.........48

Mark
4:39.............219
11:22a,
  23-24.........153

Luke 17:2.......72

John
7:24.............206
14:16-17......242

Acts
2:1-4............. 232
16:1-9.........247

Romans
8:26............. 137
8:35,
  37-39.........203

1 Corinthians
12:26b.........152

2 Corinthians
4:7-10.........199
12:7b-10......197
13:8-9.........113

Ephesians
6:5.................19

1 Timothy
2:11-15........ 246

Hebrews
3:19b.............181
6:19.............290
11:1.............143

2 Peter
2:19.............308

CPSIA information can be obtained
at www.ICGtesting.com
Printed in the USA
LVHW081723030320
648856LV00010B/706